MURD

MANSLAU   R

AROUND CANNOCK CHASE

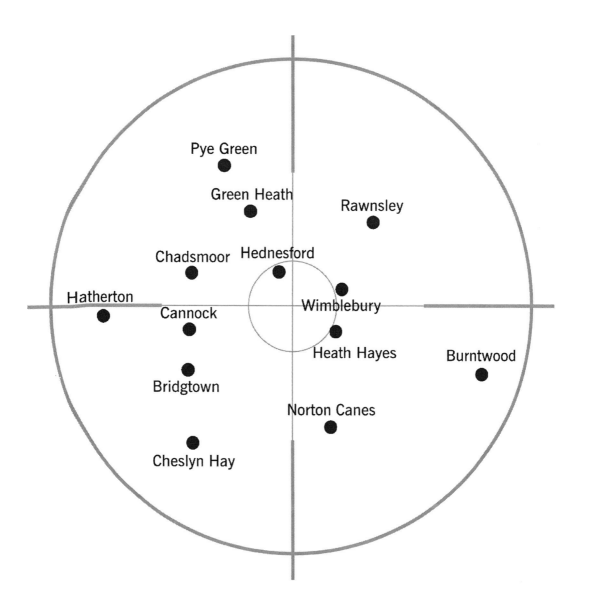

Pye Green

Green Heath

Rawnsley

Chadsmoor   Hednesford

Hatherton

Cannock

Wimblebury

Heath Hayes

Burntwood

Bridgtown

Norton Canes

Cheslyn Hay

Anthony Hunt

Published by
Mount Chase Press
109 Mount Street, Hednesford, Cannock, Staffs. WS12 4DB
01543 422891

ISBN 978-0-9551382-1-8

Designed and produced by John Griffiths, printed by 4 Edge Limited, Hockley, Essex.

Contents

List of maps

List of photographs

Acknowledgements

Many thanks to those people and societies who loaned the following photographs:-

D. Battersby for 18, 19, 20, 30, 31 and 68; Birmingham Post for 6, 46, 48, 49 and 53; Burntwood Chase Heritage Group for 13 and 14; Cannock Chase Mining Historical Society for 73; Cheslyn Hay & District Local History Society for 8, 23 and 24; Mrs. V.A. Dean for 40; Mrs. T. Dudley for 65; Mrs. P. Dutton for 26; Mrs. J. Edmunds for 27 and 28; Express & Star for 5, 16 and 59; Mr. & Mrs. Flavahan for 9 and 10; R. Fullelove for 38 and 39; F. & I. Groves for 61, 62, 63 and 64; J. James for 47; Mrs. M. Jones for 66; T. Jones for 54 and 56; Museum of Cannock Chase for 21, 22, 42, 43, 44, 45, 50, 67, 69 and 70; Norton Canes Heritage Society for 55 and 58; Mrs. Parsonage for 3 and 52; Mrs. J. Pickerill for 1, 2, 41 and 51; D. Pugh for 34; Mrs. R. Reid for 11 and 12; G. Sirdifield for 33, 35 and 36; and R. Smith for 72.

Any pictures loaned by the various local history societies and the museum were done so in the good faith that the original owners would be only too pleased to see their photographs in print.

Finally, all photographs were loaned in good faith, but apologies to anyone whose copyright may have been unintentionally infringed.

INTRODUCTION

Following the success of my recent book on *The History of Hednesford and Surrounding Villages* I thought it would be a good idea to combine my passion for local history with my other hobby – that of collecting the many Staffordshire cases of murder and manslaughter during the Victorian Era and the early part of the twentieth century. This new book, therefore, details some of the most notorious crimes from around the Cannock Chase area, ranging from Burntwood to Bridgtown, Cannock to Cheslyn Hay and Hatherton to Heath Hayes.

As with my previous murder books I have kept mainly to the period from 1840 to 1920, hoping not to open up any old wounds or uncover skeletons deeply locked away in family cupboards. However, I could not allow the book to be published without describing our only unsolved murder which happened much later – that of Elsie May Taylor from Bridgtown who was viciously killed in her own home in 1957.

In the hope of being helpful to local historians and those endeavouring to trace their own family history I have tried, where possible, to include as many names of people and places as well as producing maps of the various areas involved. That has meant that I have almost driven mad the local librarians with my incessant requests for the Census results and O.S. Maps. May I thank them for their patience.

Likewise I have pestered the local press with advertisements for photographs. Without their help and the kind donations from their many readers this book would not be half as colourful and informative as it hopefully is. Unfortunately photographs of our local police force of the time seem to be in short supply, but I am indebted to those who lent police pictures and I have gladly used them to honour their profession. These photographs have been included in the stories about the villages where the policemen served during their careers though they may not appear in the actual crime related to. Also many thanks to those local history societies who lent their photographs.

Finally, for those who discover a taste for murder and the macabre after reading this book, may I take the opportunity to promote my other books – *Accident, Manslaughter or Murder?*; *Murder Unsolved* and *Murder in Mind*. See the back of the book for further details.

FOREWORD

Since beginning my research on murder cases some ten years ago various of my preconceptions have been greatly altered. Concentrating mainly on the Victorian period I have been impressed at how often the police managed to capture the villains and solve the crimes. Remember they knew nothing about finger printing and blood grouping, both sciences only in their infancy in the early 1900's. They relied mainly on witnesses who surprisingly came forward in their droves for most cases. Despite their lack of forensic knowledge they still managed to solve over 95% of murder or manslaughter cases.

Also I was amazed at the sentences given to the guilty person. I had always believed that the Victorians had an over inflated ideal of justice which led them to be rather unforgiving towards any criminals, yet, as many of the stories in this book will prove, they were somewhat less cruel than I had expected. Death was not the only option for murder – compassion was sought in many of the cases. That was probably due to the elaborate system used to decide whether the accused should go to trial or not.

Unlike our modern system of justice there were several processes a possible murder case went through before it reached the Assize Court. The first of these was the coroner's court held in public and more often than not in one of the local inns as they were probably the only places with rooms large enough to hold a crowd. Unlike today's coroners, who only record the cause of a person's death or make judgements on treasure trove, earlier coroners went into the reasons behind a victim's death and even went so far as to name the possible suspect and pronounce on his or her guilt or innocence. To do that they were helped by a jury of local people who probably knew both victim and perpetrator.

It is worth noting here that the accused did not have to attend the coroner's hearing if he or she did not wish to do so but could remain in custody until a verdict was announced. Also he or she had the right to remain silent when in the court and did not have to answer any questions if he or she did not wish to do so. Frequently an accused did want to speak in his or her defence, but the coroner always pointed out that it could harm his or her case (much like our police do when arresting a person).

Once the coroner's court had announced its verdict the prisoner attended the magistrates' hearing. It was only the magistrates who could formally charge a prisoner with the crime; the coroner's court merely suggested the possible course of action. It was hoped that the verdict of both courts would concur, but that was not always the case. Sometimes the coroner's court could find a person innocent, but the magistrates would disagree or it could happen the other way. In that case the trail had to be sent to the Assizes held in the county town – in our case Stafford. However, most cases were relatively clear cut and the Assize Court was only used when the coroner and magistrates had pronounced a verdict of Guilty.

The following case hopefully demonstrates how the inquest system operated.

THE DEATH OF P.C. HARRY ADAMS
Norton Canes 1914

On Friday, December 12th Constable Adams left his home, the police station in Norton Canes, at around eight o'clock to patrol the streets and lanes of the village. It was a dark evening and by 9.30 p.m. he was in Norton Hall Lane which at that time had no street lamps to light it. Suddenly he was knocked over by someone on a bicycle and fell to the ground hitting his head on the road. Unfortunately the person did not stop to see if the officer was injured and he lay there for almost half an hour until Mr. Joseph Underwood found him. Mr. Underwood had been walking back from the Fleur de Lys on the Watling Street when a lorry driver had stopped him and told him of a body lying in the lane.

Once discovered P.C. Adams recovered consciousness, though he was still very groggy and disorientated. At that moment Mr. Bradburne of Swan Farm and his son arrived on the scene with the father furious and claiming that someone had attacked his son. Mr. Underwood explained that the constable had been knocked over and, looking round the road, the group discovered a bicycle lamp and soft hat which belonged to Rupert Bradburne, the son. It was then that Mr. Bradburne calmed down and offered to walk the constable home along with Mr. Underwood.

1 & 2. Swan Farm on Watling Street (A5)

As they went along the constable seemed to recover even more and when they reached his gate he insisted on walking up the garden path unaided. All seemed well, but as the days went on Mrs. Adams became worried and so sent for Dr. Butter. He examined him on December 15th and continued to treat him until December 22nd when the constable was admitted to Wolverhampton General Hospital. When he arrived he was practically unconscious and never regained consciousness, dying on December 27th. Because of the nature of the death a post mortem had to be held and that was followed by a coroner's inquest.

That inquest opened on Tuesday December 29th at Wolverhampton Town Hall in North Street before Mr. G. Maynard Martin. A jury of twelve men and two reserves had been quickly formed from men living in Lord Street, Wolverhampton and they were summoned to attend. Lord Street was right next to the hospital and therefore it was easier to use those jurors. (It was a legal obligation to attend jury service at a coroner's inquest if requested. There were cases of jurymen being fined for non-attendance or even lateness.) Also attending were the witnesses found so far as well as Rupert Bradburne, the possible perpetrator of the "crime", along with Superintendent Pillimen of the Staffordshire Police.

The first witness was Helen Mackay, house surgeon at Wolverhampton General Hospital who had been present at the post mortem on the instructions of the coroner which was carried

---

County Borough of Wolverhampton, to wit.

To the Constables and other Peace Officers of the Borough of Wolverhampton, in the County of Stafford, and to each and every of them.

By Virtue of my Office:- These are in his Majesty's Name to command and require you immediately upon sight hereof, to Summons and warn *14* good and lawful men of the said Borough, personally to appear before me, **George Maynard Martin, Esquire**, the Coroner of our said Lord and King, for the said Borough on *Tuesday* the *29th* day of *December* instant, at the Coroner's Court, Town Hall, North Street, in the said Borough, by *half past ten* of the clock, in the *fore*noon of the same day to constitute a Jury, then and there to enquire of, do and execute all such matters and things as on His Majesty's behalf shall be lawfully given them in charge, touching the death of *Harry Adams* now lying dead in the said Borough:

And you are also hereby required to summon and warn to be and appear before me at the said Inquest, at the said time and place, all Witnesses whom you may be credibly informed can give material evidence touching the said death: And be you then and there with this Warrant to make a return of the names of the persons whom you shall have so summoned; And further to do and execute such matters as shall be then and there enjoined on you.

Given under my hand and seal this *28th* day of *December*, One Thousand Nine Hundred and *Fourteen*.

G. Maynard Martin.
Coroner.

Appointed that the Coroner and Jury may not be kept waiting: and each Juryman is subject to a fine of *Forty Shillings*, in case he makes default in attending according to his summons, and the Witnesses are liable to imprisonment in case of default.

out by the hospital pathologist. She stated that when the scalp was stripped back it revealed a bruise on the back of the head. There was no fracture inside the skull, but there was a haemorrhage both inside and outside the membrane of the brain. Death in the surgeon's opinion was due to a compression in the brain caused by the injury to the back of the head.

She continued, stating that the haemorrhage might have started immediately after the blow and slowly developed and spread. It was that which could have caused the loss of memory concerning the events of the night of December 12th.

It was the next witness, Sarah Adams, wife of the constable, who could throw more light on the constable's behaviour after the tragedy. She had seen her husband between five and six on December 12th when he left the house to go to the Fleur de Lys to tell the owners that they had been granted an extension. He must have returned at about twenty minutes past seven and had a meal, though she did not see him as she was out. The next time she saw him was about twenty minutes past ten when he arrived back home. He appeared normal, taking off his uniform and going into the garden.

He then consulted his diary and said that he had a meeting at twelve o'clock, sat down and began to doze. However, when he woke he could not remember the meeting or the time of it. She told him that he must go to it and then went to bed, but at one o'clock she heard him being very sick downstairs. Not long after he came upstairs and said that he felt ill. He complained of his head and chest and while he was getting into bed he heaved all the time. He had no sleep that night, complaining of the pains in his head. When the witness asked him what had caused the pains he said that he did not know saying, "I can't understand it". Noticing mud on his cape she asked him if he had had a fall, but he could not remember.

The following morning he still complained of pains in his head and chest and lay on the sofa until half past ten. He got up, shaved, cleaned his uniform and went out to the other station in the village. When he returned he was even worse and lay down again. During the time he was lying down Rupert Bradburne called to ask how he was and the witness remembered him saying

to her daughter, "I am very sorry. It was a pure accident." After he had gone Mr. Underwood arrived to see how he was and the witness noticed how surprised her husband was when Mr. Underwood told him about finding him unconscious in the road.

By December 15th when her husband had not recovered Sarah sent for Dr. Butter and he treated him until December 22nd when he was admitted to Wolverhampton Hospital. She told the court that she visited him at the hospital, but her husband knew nothing of the "accident" nor did he seem to know her.

Questioned by the jury Sarah said that she thought the whole incident was an accident. She could not think of anyone who bore him ill will and was certain that her husband was "on good terms" with Rupert Bradburne. As to her husband she said that she had examined him a day after the incident and he had a black eye as if he had been "struck over the eyelid with a whip". Also she was certain that he was "a sober man who never got under the influence".

*Unlike the jury at an Assize Court the coroner's jury was allowed to question the witnesses as the jury was seen as part of the investigating process.

The execution of this precept or Warrant appears by the Schedule hereunder written - The answer of *Harry Marshall* Police Constable of Wolverhampton.	**Witnesses.**
	1. *Sarah Elizabeth Adams*
	2. *Rupert Bradburne*
	3. *Arthur Bradburne*
	4. *Joseph Underwood*
	5. *Dr. Helen Mackay*

Names of the Jurors summoned on this INQUEST.		**Address.**
1. *Arthur Gennoe*	Foreman	*45 Lord Street*
2. *Thomas Hopkins*		*43 ..*
3. *Albert Taylor*		*44 ..*
4. *Arthur Roberts*		*46 ..*
5. *Walter Roberts*		*47 ..*
6. *Edmund Hartsorne*		*48 ..*
7. *Samuel Stephens*		*53 ..*
8. *John Postings*		*54 ..*
9. *Charles Webb*		*55 ..*
10. *Albert Harriman*		*56 ..*
11. *George Bowers*		*59 ..*
12. *Philip Baker*		*60 ..*
Walter Turner		*61 ..*
Alfred Wiley		*62 ..*

N.B. The Coroner particularly requests that Constables will avoid repeatedly summoning the same Jurymen, and impress upon the attention of those summoned the absolute necessity of their punctual attendance at the time and place fixed by this warrant.

Facsimile of the Jurors present at the trial

The next witness was Joseph Underwood, a schoolmaster in Norton Canes. He testified that between 9.50 and 9.58 p.m. he was walking along Norton Hall Lane from the Watling Street direction and a lorry was in front of him. He noticed the lorry stop and the driver got out and walked towards him carrying a lamp. The driver told him that he had passed a policeman lying in the road and also a bicycle. Hurrying up the witness discovered P.C. Adams lying at right angles to the road and quite unconscious. His stick was about a yard from his body on the right hand side.

Very shortly the constable opened his eyes, but still seemed only semi-conscious and did not understand what had happened to him or where he was. The witness told him what had happened and also said that he was the schoolmaster. Gradually the witness raised him into a sitting position and finally to his feet, but still he was very shaky. At that point Mr. Bradburne and his son arrived on the scene and Mr. Bradburne wanted to know where the men were who had attacked his son.

Having explained what had happened to the constable they all began to examine the scene and soon found the bicycle and a soft hat. Rupert Bradburne said that the hat was his. The witness then said that he thought P.C. Adams should be taken home and the man with the dray lorry offered to take him. It was about a five minute walk away and ultimately the witness and Mr. Bradburne saw him to his gate. However, he would not let them go further and preferred to walk down the entry alone. On the Sunday the witness saw the constable and questioned him about the accident, but the constable seemed surprised and seemed to know little about it.

Questioned about the incident and in particular about Rupert Bradburne Mr. Underwood said that the lad had told him that he was riding down the lane when he saw something dark in front of him. A hand seemed to be put up as he passed, but before he knew anything else he had run into the object and knocked it over. He was sure that there had never been any ill-will between the lad and P.C. Adams and they "always seemed to be the best of friends". Finally he stressed that the lane was always very, very dark at night and that particular night was very dark.

3. Norton Police Specials 1919 - Back row - W. Read, L. Emery, P. Emery, W. Emery. Middle row - A. Rock, T. Hurmson, H. Bailey, J. Gidwell, J. Rock, C. Eccleston, W.Jones. Seated - Constable Kettle, T. Philpott, J. Taylor, Mr. Underwood, F. Smith, Constable Starling.

The final witness at that inquest was Mr. Arthur Bradburne, a farmer living at Swan Farm on the Watling Street. He stated that his son, Rupert, arrived home on December 12th about ten o'clock and could barely walk. When questioned as to what had happened his son said that as he was riding down Norton Hall Lane someone had put his arms up and pulled him off his bicycle. He had had his storm lamp over his arm and had ridden over the man. They had both fallen with the man going backwards. When asked who the man was the lad had said that he had been too shocked to wait around and just came home to fetch the witness.

The witness then told the hearing that they both ran back to the scene, but as they neared they saw a policeman standing amongst two or three other men. On arriving at the scene the witness had asked who had knocked his son off the bicycle, but on being told what had happened to the constable he took it that P.C. Adams must have been the man. Shortly after that he helped to take the constable home.

When questioned he was adamant that the constable was "the best of friends with all of his family" including his son, Rupert. However, he went on to state that his son would have been too scared to stay at the scene after the incident because he had been stopped on several occasions at night and had even been assaulted.

4. P.C. Adams's grave in St. James's Churchyard, Norton Canes.

If that were the case the coroner concluded the lad could be excused for not staying at the scene, but he would need more proof of the lad's fear. Because of that he adjourned the inquest to give time for that proof to be brought forward.

The second inquest began on Monday January 4th, 1915 with Mr. Bradburne producing a letter which he had written to the Chief Constable of Staffordshire which read:-

Dear Sir,

I am writing to you to know what can be done with regard to the treatment my son is being subjected to.

1st. On December 1st. he attended a Home Defence Drill at Lichfield. On his way home, a distance of 7 miles, someone attempted to stop him, but he got away safely.

The next morning I received a letter, my son also, warning me to stop him attending another class. My son's was similar signed "A Spy". He still attended the class and nothing happened until December 10th when he was again stopped by a man on a bicycle on a lonely part known as Wooden Stables.

Knocked over and then assaulted. But my son proved the best man, but couldn't detain him. On the 15th again stopped by 2 men who overpowered him, who carried him 145 yards across common land near Heath Hayes and Wooden Stables, bound him hands and feet and gagged him and threw him into a brook then ran away.

Fortunately he was able with his hands and feet to get on a bank and after a time he released his hands and in this position he lay for two and a half hours, seeing his friends looking for him and whistling and yet couldn't answer them. When he at last freed himself he walked home meeting us who were looking for him.

December 19th. In going round the stables tonight a very heavy brick tied to a piece of string was placed over one door. When the door opened it came down just missing his head. I was there at the time and saw this happen.

The police have it in hand here, but it is now so serious that something must be done.

Will you give it your opinion as to what should be done.

Yours truly,
A. Bradburne.

Mr. Bradburne also produced a diary which his son had been told to keep to record the various assaults and threats. Curiously it was labelled "My Adventures 1914" which might have set off alarm bells with the coroner. What follows is that diary.

> *December 1st. I was attempted to be stopped on the Watling Street near Harrisons Offices. But got away.*
>
> *Next morning I received a letter warning me to beware or send my resignation into the Home Defence Force, Lichfield. Father also received a letter.*
>
> *December 10th. I was stopped by the Wooden Stables and knocked down by a man and bicycle. We then fought, but I beat him, but could not detain him.*
>
> *December 15th. I was again stopped by the Wooden Stables and overpowered by two men who tied my hands and feet and gagged me by placing a lot of grass in my mouth and tying a piece of rag over my mouth. They then carried me 145 yards across common land and the threw me in a ditch full of water. After being in the ditch about two and a half hours I managed to get one hand loose and thus freed myself altogether.*
>
> *December 19th. Another attempt to do me in in the stables on our own farm between the hours of 7 o'clock and 9 o'clock. A brick was placed over the stable door so that when I opened it the brick came down with such force that it cut the rope down to one strand and missed me by inches.*
>
> *December 22nd. I was travelling along the Watling Street between Mr. Badger's farm and Leacroft Lane when a man came up on a bicycle and gave me a paper and said "read this". The moment I took it he stabbed me on the left side. I thought I was badly stabbed as the blow hurt me so. He immediately jumped on his bicycle and rode off before I could recover myself. I then examined my side and found he had stabbed right through my clothes and dented my ribs and I found half the knife blade sticking in my clothes.*

Reads a little like a James Bond movie. Why should an ordinary lad in an ordinary place and occupation be subjected to the spy routine? The coroner also could smell a rat and wanted young Rupert Bradburne to give his side of the story. However, as already explained, the accused did not have to say anything at an inquest. Nevertheless Rupert was only too glad to take the stand.

Having been duly warned that anything he said might be used in evidence against him at another trial Rupert was happy to begin. He stated that he was the eighteen year old son of Mr. Arthur Bradburne and helped him on the farm. At about a quarter to ten on December 12th he was riding his bicycle from Norton Canes Institute where he had been playing billiards. The evening was dark and a little foggy and he had no lamp on his bike, but carried a storm lamp on his arm. He came to the place in Norton Hall Lane where there was a slight turn to his left and was only doing five or six miles an hour.

All of a sudden he felt arms come across him and was pitched right over the handle bars on to the ground. The storm lamp went out and he could not see where he was or find the bike. He did not see the policeman, but rushed home as fast as he could to tell his father that he had been pulled off the bike.

When questioned about being pulled off the bicycle Rupert began to waver and admitted that he thought that he had been pulled up by somebody, but did not know what really had happened as it was so dark.

He continued to tell the hearing that he had gone back to the scene with his father and then saw the policeman standing amongst the men. His father had questioned the group about an assault on his son and had then been told of the incident. It was when he carried the light for his father to help the constable home that he began to realise what had really happened.

Once Rupert began to admit guilt it was as if the flood gates were opened and he started to relate how he had made up all the other stories. He said that he had not been interfered with on December 1st and he had written the anonymous letters to himself and his father. However, he was knocked down by a cyclist on December 10th, but he now believed it was accidental. As to the attack on December 15th there was "no truth in that statement". He also admitted that he placed the brick over the door on the 19th and had made up the story about the knife attack. He had found the knife on the road and cut his own clothes.

Finally, once his guilty secrets were out, he told the hearing that he could not account for his telling all the lies except that his mind might be "unhinged" because he had been worried about the War. His brother was waiting to go to the Front and he was scared that he might be called up. His father had insisted that he go to the Home Defence Drill at Lichfield and he did not like the journey to and from Lichfield as he had to travel in the dark. It was that which made him write the letters so that his father might stop him going. However, once his father sent the letters to the police he was "forced" to carry on telling lies in case his first lie was discovered.

A somewhat bemused Arthur Bradburne was recalled and was asked about his son's behaviour. He said that he was satisfied with his son's explanations concerning the alleged assaults. He then said that his son had been "excited" since the War started and when alone seemed to get "delirious". He was certain that Rupert had been "nervous" on his night rides to Lichfield and when he had come home on December 12th he was "very excited" which led the witness to believe there had been another assault.

Although the lad had obviously lied the court still had to be certain that the actual tragedy was accidental and so Superintendent William Grove was called. He produced a rough sketch of the road from Norton Canes to the Watling Street via Norton Hall Lane. He told the court that there was a steep gradient down to the tree marked on the drawing and that there was a footpath on the left which stopped just at the tree near to where P.C. Adams was found lying. He said that it was possible that Adams might have stepped off into the road and would not be visible to the cyclist. The lane was not lighted at all.

Having heard the sorry story the coroner instructed the jury to find a verdict of accidental death which they did. The jury also recommended that Rupert Bradburne be censured as to his future conduct and that a lamp be placed at the corner of the road in Norton Hall Lane. (I am told that it was.)

*I am indebted to Mr. Colin Adams, P.C. Adams's grandson, who, when tracing his family history, came across this episode and lent me all the details and the photostats of the inquest.

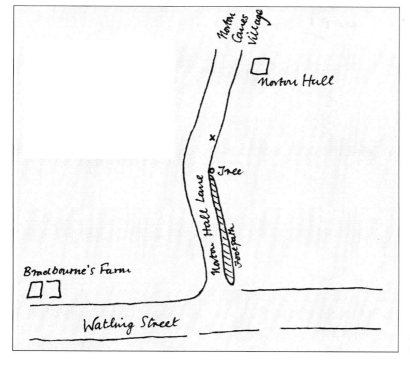

Map 1.
A copy of the rough plan of the accident scene drawn by Superintendent William Grove and presented to the coroner and jury. X marks the accident spot.

WHO KILLED ELSIE MAY?
Bridgtown 1957

It should have been just a quiet Monday morning like most starts to the week at Cannock Police Station, but as Sergeant James stood at the desk the door suddenly burst open and in raced a panicked John Holgate. Breathless and white with shock he began to blurt out something about a body which he had discovered at No. 35 Longford Road, Bridgtown. A woman was lying in her front room - a friend whom he had seen alive only about a week before.

Once quietened down, Holgate related how he had last seen the victim on Monday, April 8th, but over the weekend just gone he had called at the house several times but been unable to make anyone hear. He had called on the Friday evening, but as the curtains were drawn he had presumed that she may have gone to Stafford to visit friends. However, he had visited again on the Saturday just in case she may have arrived back home. When he went on the fatal morning he had had a terrible feeling that something dreadful may have happened and so he had forced the door and discovered the body.

5. Number 35 Longford Road.

Realising the man's obvious distress Sergeant James informed Superintendent Wall and the three men went to Longford Road. There they found the body of Elsie May Taylor, with part of a mat curled up over her legs, possibly caused when the door was forced open. The body was tied around the wrists and ankles with what looked like clothes line rope. A quick search of the rooms found her slippers nearby and her outdoor shoes in the living room. Her bag contained a purse which was empty save for a sixpence. On the table was a periodical *Silver Star* dated April 10th and a copy of the latest edition of the *Cannock Advertiser*, both presumably delivered on the Friday evening.

Without further investigation of the property the police called in the forensic team. (The police had by this time realised that vital information could be obtained from a murder scene if as little as possible was interfered with until the experts had examined the area.) They in the meantime began their own investigations into the movements of the victim on the previous weekend and involved the press quickly in the hope that as many witnesses would come forward as possible who may be able to throw some light on the case.

Eventually they were informed by the forensic team that the murder must have taken place late Friday 12th or in the early hours of the Saturday morning and so the police concentrated their efforts in tracking down Elsie May's known movements on that evening. Such was the horror of the crime that before long the police were inundated with possible witnesses so that by the time of the inquest on May 20th they had no less than thirty five people willing to testify.

That inquest was held at Cannock Police Court before the coroner Mr. K. T. Braine-

Hartnell and the first evidence heard was that of the forensic team. Dr. S. Griffiths of the Birmingham Forensic Laboratory stated that he helped in the post mortem and found lacerations to the left side of the scalp and bruises around both eyes and on the bridge of the nose. However, he found no signs of a sexual attack, but strangely there were no defensive wounds which one might expect when a victim was being tied up.

Death he estimated was due to the sudden stopping of the heart following a blow to the victim's throat or the gripping of the throat. However, he said that he could not be certain if the deceased had been strangled, but may have simply died because of the blow from, he estimated, a strong person.

Dr. F. Burke, also of the Birmingham Forensic Laboratory, stated that the body had been lying face down and fully extended. Both the wrists and ankles were tied with the knots facing backwards. There was blood on the hands, face and hair. John Merchant, also from the same laboratory, said that he had tested the blood found at the scene on the rug and found it to be Group A, the same as the victim's. He had discovered blood on the living room door, but unfortunately it was too light for him to make a test. (Today's D.N.A. would have no problem with that as even the tiniest speck can produce results!)

He also stated that when the police had discovered blood on Mr. Richard's ear (one of the original suspects) it had proved to be Group O.

Finally, Sergeant Hurmson of Stafford testified that he had taken fingerprints at the scene and examined them. He found that "except for one set, that of Mr. Harry Richards found on a partially filled gin bottle on the top of the cellar steps, they were all those of Mrs. Taylor."

★Later the police discovered another print at the scene and in an endeavour to find the culprit they fingerprinted over 300 men over 16 years of age in the Bridgtown area. They had plans to fingerprint some 16,000 more in the area, but by May 22nd the suspect print had been identified

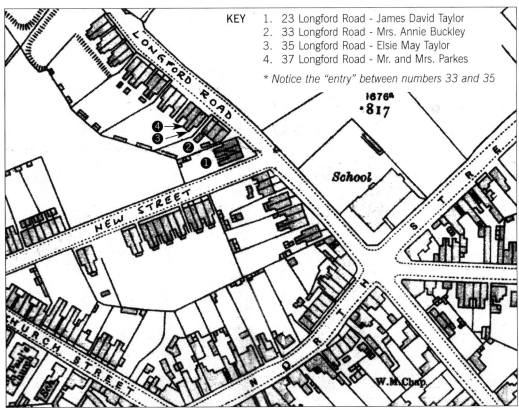

KEY
1. 23 Longford Road - James David Taylor
2. 33 Longford Road - Mrs. Annie Buckley
3. 35 Longford Road - Elsie May Taylor
4. 37 Longford Road - Mr. and Mrs. Parkes

* Notice the "entry" between numbers 33 and 35

Map 2. Bridgtown 1918.

and the person had had a valid reason for being in the house. They never named the person! Was it one of their own investigators, I wonder?

All three pathologists were in agreement that the time of death was sometime between the hours of late on the evening of Friday April 12th and during the early hours of Saturday April 13th. What followed then at the inquest was a series of witnesses who could possibly throw light on Elsie May's final movements before the crime.

First to appear was Joseph Thacker, a tallyman who lived at Walsall Wood Road, Aldridge. He called at the victim's home every Friday evening to collect instalments on carpets and clothing that Elsie May had purchased previously. He told the hearing that he had arrived at No. 35 Longford Road some time between 7.15 p.m. and 7.30 p.m. on Friday 12th. He went into the living room where a fire had just been lit. The deceased was wearing a black skirt and a sweater. She had paid him the usual £1 and he thought that she may have had three to five more pound notes in her purse. She appeared perfectly normal in her attitude.

Mrs. Annie Buckley, who lived at No. 33, stated that she had known the deceased all her life and for the last two years had lived next door to her. She had last seen Elsie May at 6.30 p.m. on the Friday and at 8.00 p.m. she had noticed coal being delivered to No. 35 though she did not see the deceased at that time. She had noticed that the house curtains were drawn which was unusual for that time of night. She had gone to bed around 10.30 p.m. and had heard nothing from next door all night. She told the court that she was a light sleeper and was sure she would have woken if there had been a disturbance next door. If she had not woken her dog would have barked if he had heard noises. She also said that she had not even heard the deceased arrive home at 11.15 p.m.

*What must be made clear is that there was an entry between numbers 33 and 35 and so Mrs. Buckley possibly missed some of the noises despite her being such a light sleeper.

Mr. and Mrs. Parkes from No. 37 Longford Road testified that they had arrived home from a night out on the fatal evening at around 10.45 p.m. and had stayed up until about midnight. They had heard nothing from No. 35 that evening though usually they could hear the deceased coughing or even moving about "in her normal way" as the walls were so thin. However, their dog had barked and woken them up at around 3.00 a.m. on the Saturday morning.

Next to give evidence was Eric Raymond Wilkes, the deceased's brother. He told the hearing that he and his wife had been out to Saredon on the Friday evening and had driven back passed his sister's at around 10.15 p.m. He was sure of the time because he had noticed that the curtains were all drawn and the lights were on upstairs and downstairs at the house and he had said to his wife, "Looks as if Elsie May is still up."

On the Saturday morning Samuel Isaac Powell, the breadman who lived at 9 Cross Street, Hazel Slade, went to No.35 to deliver the usual order. He found the back door locked which was unusual (it was his usual practise just to knock and then go in) and so he knocked loudly. As there was no answer he put the loaf on the scullery window ledge and left. When he returned on the Monday morning the bread was still there and, presuming that the deceased was away, he took the loaf away. Under questioning he said that he had not noticed whether the curtains were drawn or not.

6. Superintendent F. Wall and Detective Superintendent E. Hulme at Cannock Police Station.

Emily Kingston, sister-in-law to the deceased, also visited the house on that Saturday morning. She told the court that her son usually delivered magazines to Elsie May on Fridays during his paper round, but on that weekend he was ill and so she had done his delivery the following morning. She was certain that she had delivered the *Silver Star* at 9.00 a.m., but as she could make no one hear she pushed it under the door. Under questioning she said that she could not imagine how it had come to be found on the table in the living room when the police searched the house on the Monday. Had Holgate moved it when he forced his way into the house and simply forgotten all about it in his panic? Seems to be the only logical explanation.

During their investigations the police had quickly ruled out burglary even though some money had gone missing. Gertrude Emberton of Exeter Street, Stafford had told them that Mrs. Taylor worked with her at English Electric in Stafford and usually bought savings stamps from her on Thursdays after she had been paid. Her wage was £6 and she often had as many as eight half crown stamps. (Half a crown was 2s 6d in old money). That particular week the witness had left eight stamps in Mrs. Taylor's desk on the Friday and they had gone. She presumed the deceased had taken them. The police had not discovered them in their search of No. 35.

There was also the missing money from the deceased's purse. Remember Mr. Thacker had seen pounds notes in her purse, but Sergeant James had only found a sixpence there. However, the police discarded that theory as the were no signs of a break-in or rummaging around in the house. Burglars usually cause damage when trying to find valuables. They believed that whoever had committed the crime took the money just to make it look like burglary. Instead the police were soon led to believe that the motive for murder was sex and the perpetrator was a close friend or relative. Their investigations then began to concentrate on those close to Elsie May.

*Random killing is rare and police know that around 95% of all murders involve money or sex. The latter is most often committed by someone the victim knows, either a close relative or acquaintance.

By the time of the inquest three possible suspects had been identified and they were to give evidence during the remainder of the hearing.

The first of those was James David Taylor, the ex-husband of Elsie May, although they had never divorced. He told the hearing that he lived at 23 Longford Road and worked as an edge tool maker. He had married Elsie May on December 24th, 1943, but they had no children. About seven years ago his wife had got a job at a Bridgtown shop where she got to "know" Holgate. About two years ago he, the witness, had asked her to leave him and she did without any argument. She had then gone to live with her father at No. 35, but he had since died.

7. Wedding of Elsie May and James Taylor, December 24th 1943.

Over the last two years there had been several "words" with Holgate about the relationship with his ex-wife, but it had never turned into any "serious bother". As he told the hearing, "After so long I took no notice of it and let her go her own way and I went mine." He also knew Harry Richards, another suspect, but he had not known that he was seeing his ex-wife until six months ago. Finally, he said that they had split on friendly terms and Elsie May had never made any maintenance claim against him; she preferred to look after herself.

As to the night in question he testified that he had helped a local butcher that evening until

8.00 p.m. and had then gone to the Four Crosses Inn at Hatherton where he stayed all evening. At closing time he took a friend home to Saredon and got back to his own home at about 11.00 p.m. On the Saturday he worked in the butcher's shop until 2.30 p.m. On the Sunday he got up around 10.30 a.m. and went out for a drink at about 12 noon.

★The police had checked his alibi and all the details were backed up by witnesses and so James Taylor was considered less of a suspect than the following two witnesses who appeared at the inquest.

The first of those was Harry Richards of 463 Wolverhampton Road, Cannock who was a poultry farmer. He informed the court that he had known the deceased for a number of years, but after her father's death he had not seen her for about eighteenth months. Then she had telephoned him and they had started to go out together drinking about twice a week and he had visited her home on several occasions. It was not long into their relationship that they became intimate.

On the fatal evening he had picked her up around 8.20 p.m. and they had gone to the Wolseley Arms just outside Rugeley. They had left the public house around 10.30 p.m. and driven across Cannock Chase where they tried to have sex at the German Cemetery, but failed. They arrived back at the deceased's home around 11.15 p.m., but he did not go in. He then went home and went to bed not long after. He did not bother going to see her on the Saturday as it was usual for Elsie May to go to the hairdresser's that day, but he did go around on Sunday at 1.10 p.m. to pick her up for her driving lesson. He knocked the door, but when there was no answer he simply drove away.

Under questioning Richards admitted that he had been into No. 35 about three times. About seven weeks previous to the dreadful weekend he had given Elsie May a bottle of gin which would account for his fingerprint being on the bottle. As to the night when he called for her he told the court that he could not remember if the curtains were drawn or if the lights were on.

When questioned about the deceased's relationship with Holgate which had been still going on when he was seeing her, Richards said

that he was "not bothered" and there had never been any trouble concerning it.

During their investigations the police had interviewed people to check Richards's story, especially that concerning the Friday evening. The first to give evidence was Dorothy Richards, Harry's wife. She stated that he had gone out on the Friday between eight and nine o'clock, though he had not said where he was going. She had gone to bed at 11.10 p.m. and had heard him arrive back home at about 11.20 p.m. He had come to bed shortly after having a cup of tea and had not left the house for the rest of the night. He was still in bed when she woke the next morning and seemed terribly shocked when she broke the news to him about the murder on the Monday.

As to the evening spent at the Wolseley Arms Flight Lieutenant Wardragh testified that he was in the public house on Friday April 12th at 9.15 p.m. and had seen the deceased with a man whom he later identified as Harry Richards. They had been at the inn on previous occasions. However, he particularly noticed them that evening as they did not seem to be enjoying themselves like everyone else. There was entertainment on, a dog doing tricks, and everyone was having a good time. He noticed the deceased push a £1 towards the man, but he simply pushed it back. They left some time after 10.00 p.m.

Sergeant Hanson of Stafford told the court that he was driving across Cannock Chase on the Friday evening and he passed a car at Brocton at about 10.43 p.m. heading towards the German Cemetery. The car stopped and he overtook it. He noticed that the driver was a woman whom he later identified as the deceased.

Harry Richards's alibi seemed waterproof, but what of the third suspect? He was none other than John Holgate himself - the very man who had first informed the police of the terrible crime. He would not be the first or indeed the last murderer to try and throw the police off the scent by being the one who told them of the crime.

At the inquest John Harper Holgate, a colliery fireman living at 284 Walsall Road, Great Wyrley, told the hearing that he had known the deceased

8. Hawkin's Cricket Team of 1960. John Holgate is seated on the far right on the bench.

for seven years and, despite both of them being married, they had become intimate. Eventually her husband had asked her to leave and she had moved in with her father. The witness had continued to visit her at her home most weeks on Mondays, Wednesdays, Saturdays and Sundays. Even when she began to see Harry Richards he still saw her and, despite her new relationship, it did not cause any problems.

As to the fatal weekend he told the court that he had gone to Elsie May's house on Friday April 12th at about 7.00 p.m., but she was not in. He went round to the back of the house, but the door was locked and there were no lights on. He then went to his father's house and stayed there until around 10.10 p.m. when it was time for him to go to work. On his way to work at Mid Cannock Colliery he drove passed Elsie May's house, but it was still in darkness. He arrived at work at about 10.20 p.m. and worked all night until 6.40 to 6.50 a.m. on the Saturday morning when he came up from the pit bottom. He then had a bath at the pit and went to the canteen before going to his spare time job in Heath Hayes at Tennants Bakery. He arrived there at about 8.40 a.m. and delivered bread and cakes around the Heath Hayes area till 10.00 a.m.

On his way back from the bakery he called once more at the deceased's house, around 10.10

9. G.H. Tennant's grandfather, William Tennant, and family who opened the first bakery in Heath Hayes. William eventually had six boys and one girl, Elizabeth.

a.m., but still found no one in. He noticed the bread and milk outside and the curtains still drawn and so he presumed that she was out and drove away. He drove passed again at about 4.30 p.m. on the Saturday, but the curtains were still drawn. On the Sunday morning at about 10.15 a.m. he once more drove passed, but nothing had changed.

Finally, on the Monday morning he went yet again at 8.00 a.m. and still could get no answer. However, on seeing three bottles of milk outside he became worried and so contacted Elsie May's

13

workplace in Stafford. When he was told that she had not arrived for work he returned to the house and broke in, stumbling over the corpse. He immediately went home, told his wife what had happened, informed the pit that he was going to the police station and why and then went to Cannock Police Station.

It is safe to say that John Holgate was the chief suspect and the police checked very carefully on his story. However, there were witnesses who would swear in court to having been with Holgate on the Friday evening and Saturday morning.

The first of those was Cyril Evans, an overman at Mid Cannock Colliery who lived at Bevan Lee Road, Cannock. He testified that he had seen Holgate at the colliery at around 10.15 p.m. on the Friday evening and again at 10.45 p.m. He was certain that he had travelled with him on the coach to Leacroft Colliery, Great Wyrley and had spoken with him on the telephone at 11.15 p.m. when they had reached the pit bottom. From 11.30 p.m. until 3.00 a.m. he was constantly with him down the pit and he finally spoke to Holgate at 6.00 a.m. when they were still down the pit.

Under questioning he was adamant that John Holgate could not have left the pit bottom that evening without him knowing.

The next to give evidence was Thomas Morris of 303 Stafford Road, Cannock. He testified that when he had got down the pit at Leacroft at 11.00 p.m. Holgate was already there. He was certain of that because it was up to Holgate to delegate work to him that shift. He was also sure that he had seen Holgate again two or three times during the shift and at 6.50 a.m. they had been in the cage together leaving the pit bottom. Lastly, he saw Holgate again in the canteen at Mid Cannock and he was still in his working clothes.

As to Holgate's whereabouts on leaving Mid Cannock Colliery Mr. G. H. Tennant, the manager of Tennants Bakery at Heath Hayes, stated that he saw him at 8.35 a.m. at the bakery just before Holgate left for his round. As far as Mr. Tennant was concerned Holgate appeared "quite normal".

All the witnesses having testified the coroner had no option but to declare that Elsie May

10. Elizabeth Tennant's wedding to George Burgwin outside the old Talbot Inn. Bill Tennant, son of William, is on the far right.

Taylor had been murdered by "person or persons unknown" and instructed the police to continue their investigations in the hope that they would find whoever had committed the dreadful crime.

John Holgate remained the chief suspect so far as the police were concerned and they continued to question him, hoping they might find flaws in his statements. Rumours did spread in the area about his activities while at work. One gentleman who was nineteen at the time and worked at Leacroft told me that lots of his workmates were sure that Holgate had the opportunity to commit the crime as he was often seen in the works canteen when he should have been down the pit, especially on a Friday night. He also told me that on several occasions the police arrived at Leacroft Colliery and went down the pit just hoping to catch Holgate in the wrong place at the wrong time. They never did!

Eventually investigations petered out as no new leads came forward. The murder still remains one of those very few unsolved cases on police books.

So who might have killed Elsie May? In trying to solve a murder or any crime the police take two key factors into consideration – Motive and Opportunity. So what about the three suspects in the case?

Harry Richards seems to come off best. As to motive, surely he had the best of both worlds – a wife who obviously loved him dearly (but one who loved him so much she might lie about him being in bed all night, I don't think so) and a lover whom he saw often. As to opportunity, he had very little time to get Elsie May's home, kill her and then arrive at his own house by 11.20 p.m. Remember the police sergeant who was so positive about the time he saw them near the German Cemetery.

And what of James Taylor, the estranged husband? Unfortunately he has the best opportunity of all three as he has no alibi between the murder hours. But would a man who had ignored his wife's unfaithfulness for seven years suddenly want to commit murder? The motive is poor. There was no evidence of any rows between husband and wife; they had simply decided to ignore one another.

That brings us to John Holgate. The motive could be that he was jealous of Elsie May's new relationship with Richards and so decided to confront her on the fatal evening. An argument arose (which neither neighbour overheard) and he killed her. But what of opportunity? If he did leave the pit bottom and head for Bridgtown he took an awful risk that no one would want him while he was away (he would have had to be gone for about an hour at least). Yet we have those rumours that he did leave the pit bottom at times. Was he testing out his chances?

You can perhaps see why the police had real difficulties with the case and why it has remained unsolved.

Footnote:- Stories I have heard from villagers in the Bridgtown area talked of the volatile temper that Holgate possessed. Joe Cadman, a clerk at the mine, related how Holgate was caught at work attacking a workmate. He had his hands gripped around the man's neck and had to be restrained by other men. Many of the villagers were sure that he was Elsie May's killer and that is why, when several years later he was killed in a motorbike accident with a bus, they proclaimed that he had got what he deserved.

11. Sergeant Painter c.1930 outside Bridgtown Police Station on the Walsall Road.

12. The Painter family c.1940 - The back yard at Mill Street. Back row, left to right - Jim, Sergeant Painter, Gladys, Jeff, Dorothy and Fred Hawkesworth. Front row, left to right - Francis, unknown, Mrs. Painter, Muriel.

ITCHING TO BE RID OF HIM
Burntwood 1843/44

Having lodgers is never easy. Whether relations or total strangers your house is never your own and tempers quite naturally become strained at times. Worse then when there may be a suspicion that something untoward is happening between the lodger and a member of your family. Even worse when it could be your spouse.

For eight years the Westwoods in the small village of Burntwood had been forced through financial necessity to take in lodgers (they had a growing family, eight children in all). The one lodger was Thomas Hall, a middle aged labourer, who had lived with them for a few years and the other was Samuel Phillips, a young nailer, who had been with them for almost eight years though he did not work with John, but elsewhere in the village. At first all was well and the Westwoods, Sarah and John, seemed happily married, but rumours gradually began to spread in the small community that Sarah was having an affair with her younger lodger and that perhaps some of the children were not fathered by John.

1841 CENSUS for BURNTWOOD		
John Westwood	38	Nailer
Sarah Westwood	40	
Mary Westwood	17	
Charles ..	14	Nailer
Elizabeth ..	12	
Harriet ..	10	
Eliza ..	8	
Josiah ..	5	
Anne ..	3	
John ..	2 months	
Samuel Phillips	35	Nailer

Inevitably the gossip reached John's ears and arguments between him and his wife became more frequent as did rows between John and Samuel Phillips. Stories were even told that on occasions John had attacked Phillips and Sarah had stepped in to stop the fights threatening to leave her husband if he continued his behaviour. She always hotly denied any wrong-doings and refused to send the young lodger packing. To keep her John always gave in, though the situation became increasingly fragile. No one was happy, but who could have foreseen the tragedy that was about to happen?

On the morning of Thursday, November 9th 1843 John was seen in his nailer's workshop next to the cottage between eleven and twelve o'clock and seemed in perfectly good health. At midday he returned to the cottage with his son, Charles, for some dinner and having eaten a meal of gruel (a mixture of vegetables, oatmeal, milk and water and meat) with the remainder of the family he soon complained of feeling ill. Throughout that afternoon he continued to complain of being ill and retired to bed. Although he became progressively worse Sarah did not send for a doctor, preferring to look after her husband herself or so she told the neighbours. Unfortunately John never recovered and died later that same day just before half past nine in the evening.

Strangely nothing might have been thought about the death had it not been for Sarah's unusual behaviour during the following few days. When asked about her husband's death she seemed too casual telling people that she had seen him "ten times worse on many an occasion". Even the day after she had told neighbours that she did not want to speak of it further. What seemed to them even more cold-hearted was that on the very next day she was seeking out the registrar to get a death certificate.

★ It was not unusual for burials to take place quickly after death, especially if the deceased died near to the weekend, as tradition among the working classes had it that burials took place on a Sunday and Sarah had only a few days to organise it.

However, rumours had already begun to circulate as to the probable cause of John's death. Some alleged that he had died of a broken heart because of his wife's relationship with Samuel Phillips while others openly stated that he had been poisoned. Soon those rumours reached the ears of the local gentry and constabulary and it was deemed expedient to prevent the quick burial and instigate an inquiry into the death of John Westwood. Consequently Sarah was refused a death certificate and an inquest was arranged for the following Monday.

That inquest began on Monday, November 13th at the Star Inn, Burntwood Green before Mr. Thomas Moss Phillips, the Staffordshire coroner. The jury were sworn in and all proceeded to the Westwood cottage to view the deceased's remains. That done they returned to the Star and the hearing commenced.

The first witnesses were Charles Bailey and Thomas Hall who stated that they had both seen the deceased in his workshop on the fatal morning between eleven and twelve and he seemed in perfect health. They also told the court of the intimacy between Sarah Westwood and the lodger, Phillips, and of the quarrels over the affair. Hall went on to add that despite being a lodger at the Westwood's he had not been informed of the illness by Sarah, but by the ten year old daughter who merely said that her father was "very ill". Having been told that he went into the cottage to inquire about the deceased with the next door neighbour, Mrs. Dawson, and was surprised to find Sarah sitting downstairs by the fire. He and Mrs. Dawson went upstairs to see the deceased at about nine o'clock and Westwood died half an hour later. Mary Dawson testified that she agreed with Hall's evidence as to seeing John Westwood in his shop between eleven and twelve and his appearing to be in very good health. She added that when they went upstairs at about nine o'clock the deceased was lying in a dark room and had no covering on him at all save for his night clothes. Sarah Westwood was downstairs and seemed unconcerned.

The next witness was seventeen year old Charles Westwood who told the hearing that he had been at work with his father that morning and that at about twelve o'clock they had gone to dinner. Unlike the rest of the family he had had potatoes and meat for his meal and his mother had had only a drink of tea. He had

13. The Star Inn c.1900

14. The Blue Ball Inn, Burntwood c.1910.

visited his father several times during the afternoon and witnessed him being sick on several occasions. His mother had taken the vomit downstairs and thrown it away.

Under questioning he said that it was his mother's decision not to call a doctor as she preferred to look after John herself. However, he did add that his father had complained of feeling unwell during the morning in the workshop.

Samuel Phillips was next to give evidence and he stated that he had lived with the Westwoods for about eight years and was certain that the relationship between the Westwoods was on "good terms". He denied that he and the deceased had ever quarrelled about Sarah and hotly denied any supposed affair. He also stated that John had frequently complained about feeling unwell and frequently had gruel for his dinner. As to the day in question he said that he was at work all day and only found out about the deceased's illness in the evening. He then, at the request of Mary Dawson, had fetched Robin Westwood, the deceased's brother, but shortly after they arrived back John died.

It was at that stage in the inquest that the coroner decided to adjourn until the results of the post mortem were known and also to allow the local constabulary to gain further information. That second inquest began on Monday, November 20th.

Robert (Robin) Westwood was the first to be examined. He told the hearing that he had arrived at his brother's home around eight thirty on the fatal evening. The deceased was speechless and dying. He also said that he was aware of Sarah's cohabiting with Phillips and the arguments over the affair. On one occasion, October 19th, he was present when an argument broke out about Sarah going out with Phillips the night before. His brother had asked Sarah to go with him to a tea drinking at the Ball Inn, Burntwood, but she had refused. His brother had then intimated that she would go if it were not with him, meaning she would go with Phillips, adding that "if she did not know better he would teach her better". He, Robert, had actually told Sarah that she ought not to go out without her husband and she had cursed him and said that she still would.

Next was Eliza Westwood, an intelligent ten year old daughter of the Westwoods. However, before she was asked to give evidence she was examined as to her suitability to understand the proceedings. Having satisfied the coroner that she understood about oaths and giving evidence she was sworn in and allowed to speak. She told the hearing that on the Thursday her father had gone to his work after breakfast and then returned for his dinner at midday and was "very well then". Her mother had made gruel for the family and Charles had had potatoes and meat. She had watched her mother make the meal and put the oatmeal in the kettle.

While her father was eating she overheard him ask her mother, "What's this that's white like flour in my gruel?" Her mother had replied, "I don't know." She did not see any white in her own gruel or that of her sister's food. After the meal her father had said that he felt starved and ill and so he went to bed. Also after the meal she usually washed up, but on that day her mother washed the dishes. She then left the house and went to her uncle Robin's where she stayed until nearly four o'clock. When she returned home she saw her father and he was very ill and being sick. She remembered seeing her mother bringing down some stuff in a bowl and throwing it away.

The coroner then recalled Mary Dawson who had informed the local constable that she had further information. She then testified that on the day after the death Sarah had told her that she had been to the registrar in Lichfield for the death certificate, but "she may as well have stopped at home as he would not grant her one". Sarah had then asked Mary on the Friday to go to William Stretton (the parish clerk) to "talk him out of one". It seemed to the witness that Sarah was anxious not to have an inquest and wanted to bury her husband as speedily as possible. Her excuse had been that a coroner might not arrive until late the next week and she did not want the body in the house all that time. However, since that conversation the witness had had other ideas concerning Sarah's motives.

★That sort of evidence would never be allowed in a modern court as it is merely conjecture and not evidence. Courts only deal with facts!

The final witness was Mr. Charles Allen Chevasse, a Lichfield surgeon who had performed the post mortem on Tuesday, November 14th at the Westwood home in the presence of Doctor Rowley and one of the deceased's brothers. He said that he had known the deceased some time as he had treated him for typhus the year before. He testified that the corpse was still in a perfect state of preservation at the time and that there were no external marks of bruising or violence and that it was "the healthiest subject he had ever examined". However, the stomach and bowels were "in an intense state of recent inflamation". Having analysed the stomach contents he had found a large quantity of white arsenic and he was certain that it was that which had caused death.

It should be stated that the Victorians were in the habit of taking arsenic for various illnesses and doctors carried it in their bags all the time. It was even rumoured that the Royal Family frequently took the medicine to ward off illness or possible assassination attempts. However, it was the quantity which could prove fatal and Chevasse stressed that in his evidence.

All the evidence heard Sarah was given the opportunity to have her say and she stoutly declared her innocence. The jury were not satisfied and after a few minutes deliberation they returned a verdict of "wilful murder" against Sarah. On hearing the verdict Sarah remained "unmoved" and merely said, "I'm innocent, but I reckon, sir, you'll take bail." However, her attitude changed drastically when the coroner announced that the court would not and that she was to be transported to Stafford Gaol to await the next Assizes.

★While Sarah was languishing in gaol John Westwood's funeral took place on November 22nd, 1843 and he was buried in the churchyard of Christ Church, Burntwood, the service being conducted by Reverend Ralph Essington, the incumbent vicar.

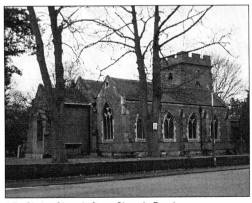

15. Christ Church from Church Road.

Her trial began on January 2nd, 1844 before Mr. Justice Baron Rolfe and because of its very nature (women accused of murder were and still are quite rare) it had attracted the notice of the local press who followed the proceedings carefully. Both the *Staffordshire Advertiser* and *Wolverhampton Chronicle* printed full details of the trail.

Mr. Corbett for the Prosecution briefly narrated the main circumstances of the sad affair and then proceeded to call his witnesses, the first being Charles Westwood. Once more Charles related the events of that fatal morning, but added further details. He was then sure that his father had complained of a pain in his head during the morning. At dinner, which he ate with his father and his three youngest sisters, Eliza, Elizabeth and Anne, he had had fried potatoes and meat and a little fried bread while all the others had had the gruel. His father had also eaten a little bread and meat. His sister, thirteen year old Harriet, had been at home at dinner time but had not eaten with them and had gone out during the meal. After their meal his father had asked one of the girls to fetch the Bible so that he might read. He had done that two or three days before, but rarely before that.

The witness had then left the house and when he returned at about one o'clock his father had gone to bed. However, he did not go to see him until around five o'clock when he asked if he was going to get up. His father had said that he "felt cold and chilly". He remembered that at around three o'clock his mother had gone upstairs and returned with the chamber pot. His father had been sick and she threw away the contents into the sough near the door. He next went to his father's bedroom at about nine o'clock with his mother and his father died about ten minutes later.

Under questioning from Mr. Yardley for the Defence Charles stated that so far as he knew his father and mother "lived on good terms" and he knew nothing of the supposed relationship between his mother and the lodger, Phillips. He had lodged with them for about seven years and on the day he had gone to work and returned between 5 and 7 o'clock. As to the actual day he was adamant that his father had complained of feeling ill before dinner. In fact he stated that his father had left the workshop on several occasions

through illness. If he was ill, which was once or twice a month for several years, he was in the habit of lying down after dinner. He added that at eight o'clock in the evening he had overheard his mother asking if she should send for a doctor and his father had refused to let her. That was before the neighbours had suggested it. In fact, he stated, it was Mary Dawson who said that it was no use sending for one. His mother had also offered to light a fire in the bedroom and took up some embers, but they had gone out.

As to the meal Charles told the court that his mother was in the constant habit of taking tea for dinner and that his father often lay down after dinner. Finally, he added, his mother had brought down the chamber pot in full view of all present and threw the contents in the usual place.

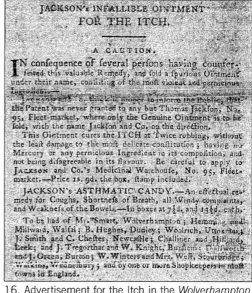

16. Advertisement for the Itch in the *Wolverhampton Chronicle* 1800.

The judge then asked Charles a question concerning the "itch" (a type of skin complaint or rash often around the genitals or just a blood disorder which caused itching) which confused the lad and he had to admit that he had never heard of the disease and to his knowledge had never suffered from it. All would become clearer later in the trial.

The next witness was ten year old Eliza who simply related her evidence given at the coroner's hearing. She did add that she was sure that she saw her mother put sugar and butter from the pantry into her father's gruel while she and her other sisters only had the sugar. As to the washing of the dishes she said that sometimes she washed up, other times one of the sisters and at other times her mother. She also said that she had seen her mother take more gruel up to her

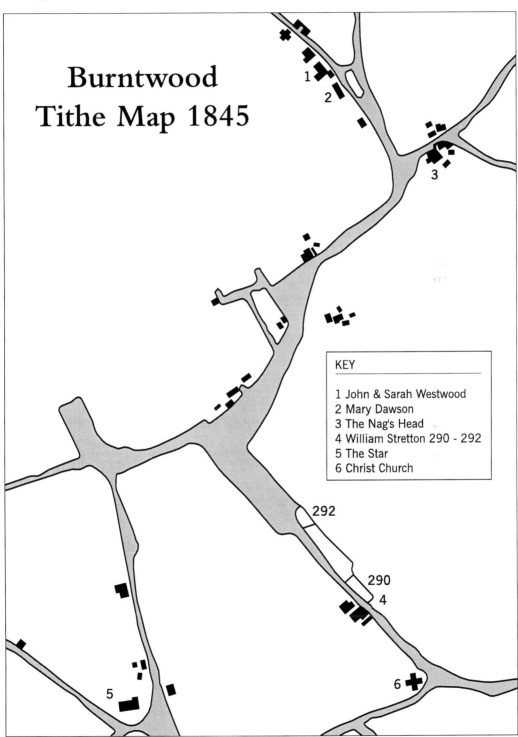

Burntwood
Tithe Map 1845

KEY

1 John & Sarah Westwood
2 Mary Dawson
3 The Nag's Head
4 William Stretton 290 - 292
5 The Star
6 Christ Church

Map 3. By kind permission of Lichfield Record Office.

father at about tea time and later saw her mother bring down a cup and saucer and the basin which had contained the gruel. She also saw her mother bring down the pot with something in it which her mother threw away.

Under questioning she said that no one had told her what to say. When the judge asked her also about the "itch" she said that she had never had it or "any breaking out on her hands".

Mary Dawson was next to take the stand and she repeated her evidence given at the inquests, adding little extra save that so far as she knew the prisoner and the deceased were "apparently on good terms" and that she had never heard the rumours about the lodger, Phillips. She had lived next door to them, only about twenty yards away, for two or three years. When she too was questioned about the "itch" she said that she did not know whether any of the Westwood family had suffered from the complaint.

The Prosecution then moved to the relationship between the prisoner and the lodger obviously to provide a possible motive for murder. Robert Westwood repeated his testimony about the evening of October 19th and the row in his brother's house. He also added further details about rows between his brother and sister-in-law.

Some time in the previous August Phillips and Sarah had taken ale from the house to take to Mr. Ashwell's at Farewell to drink while they were reaping. John, suspicious that that was not the reason for taking the ale, tackled Sarah about it in the lane behind Robert's house. Overhearing the row the witness went out and was followed back into the house by Sarah and her son, Charles. John then entered and accused her of taking the ale for other reasons to which she replied that it was not true and she would still go reaping with Phillips to earn money for the winter. He replied that she should not go with Phillips any more and left the house. Sarah and Charles stayed with the witness all that night.

William Dawson, Mary's brother-in-law, who also lived in Burntwood, told the court that he was present on September 2nd when there was a quarrel between the deceased, Phillips and Sarah Westwood in the road at Burntwood. Phillips was on the ground and John Westwood was on

17. Christ Church from Farewell Lane.

top of him. The deceased had said to Phillips, "Damn your eyes, what was you doing with her when I knocked you down!" Sarah had replied, "Damn your eyes. Kill him!" The deceased had then turned to his wife and said, "What were you doing when I knocked him down?" He continued saying, "I have catched you. I watched you last night, but I could not drop on you." Defiantly Sarah had shouted that she would beg for bread from door to door sooner than live with him (the deceased). She said that she would take her child and told her daughter, Anne, to get her bonnet and shawl.

Under cross-examination Dawson insisted that he thought Sarah was speaking to Phillips when she shouted "Kill him!", meaning that she wanted the lodger to kill her husband.

Charles Dawson, Mary's husband, stated that he was present during a quarrel between the deceased and his wife at last year's harvest time in a lane below their house. They were all sitting on a bank when Sarah suddenly struck the witness and then laid hold of her husband with one hand and struck him with the other. She shouted at her husband, "Damn your eyes, do you want to kill the man (Phillips)!" The deceased had replied that he did not but merely wanted "nothing but a right thing and a right thing he would have". The prisoner then hit the witness again saying, "This is all through you," to which he replied that it was her fault and hit her back which knocked her down. They then got up and left her on the bank. He also told the court that he had overheard many quarrels in which the prisoner had wished her husband dead.

Under cross-examination Dawson said there were many others who had witnessed such quarrels including the one in the lane.

The Prosecution did not think it worthwhile to parade more witnesses to prove the poor relationship as they had more damning evidence to introduce. Francis Richards, assistant to Mr. Heighway, a Walsall chemist, testified that he had seen the prisoner in his master's shop on November 1st, 1843 with one Hannah Mason. Hannah was well known for her "cures" and she had asked Mr. Heighway for white precipitate, red precipitate, arsenic and hellibore as a cure for the "itch". Mr. Heighway served her with a quarter of a pound of helebore powder, two pennyworth of red precipitate, two pennyworth of white precipitate and two pennyworth of arsenic (about a quarter of an ounce). She received the powders and, as instructed by the chemist, mixed them together before leaving the shop.

The following Wednesday, November 8th, the prisoner came to the shop alone and asked for the same articles she had before. She named each one and asked for them separately. The witness refused to supply the arsenic separately saying it was poisonous, but Mr. Heighway said it would be fine as she had had it before with Hannah Mason. The witness then made up the prescription with the arsenic separate, but labelled it "Arsenic - poison". He believed she had four pennyworth which was half an ounce.

Under cross-examination Richards said that it was Hannah who first used the term "itch", but when the prisoner returned she also used it. He was quite sure that was what was said and not merely "an eruption of the skin". As to Hannah Mason he confirmed that she was a frequent visitor to the shop and often made ointments for local people. The prisoner he had only seen on those two occasions.

Mr. Heighway confirmed his assistant's evidence, adding that it was Mason who first asked for the "cure for that good woman", meaning the prisoner, but it was the prisoner who paid for the powders.

Hannah Mason, an elderly Walsall woman, was next to the witness stand. Because of her age and being unwell at the time of the trial she was allowed to sit. She said that she had known the prisoner for some years and knew where she lived as her son, Samuel Phillips, lived there. She remembered that on November 1st Sarah had called at her house in Walsall and had asked her if she knew of a cure for the "itch". Having said that she did she then accompanied the prisoner to the chemist's to buy the ingredients. Nothing was said of the ingredients needed until they got to the shop. On the way to the shop she had asked how many persons needed the cure and was told there were three. Once purchased the powders were mixed and given to Sarah. She did not go back with Sarah the following week.

Under cross-examination she said that she had frequently used that preparation in the past as it would "cure the rankest itch that ever was".

Nineteen year old Mary Westwood, the eldest daughter but one, testified that she had not lived at home for over two years as she had been in service in Lichfield, but had visited home on several occasions. She spoke of the awkward situation when she was last at home between her mother, father and the lodger, Phillips. She said that on many occasions her father had wanted Phillips to leave, but her mother had threatened to leave also if he were turned out. She had returned home to live since her father's death. She told the court that she had visited her mother in the prison and her mother had said that the poison was bought to cure "a breaking out on her body and on her father's".

Under questioning Mary said that her older sister, Ann Craddock, had not been back home since her marriage which was some eighteen months ago. (Although not explicitly stated Mary inferred that was because of the awkward situation in the house.) Ann was the child who had been born before her mother and father married.

The next witness was Inspector John Raymond, in charge at Shenstone. He said that the prisoner had been put into his charge on November 20th, 1843 and on conveying her to prison she said ----.

At that point Mr. Yardley for the Defence interrupted protesting that anything said on that journey was inadmissible because his client had not been warned of the consequences of such a statement. However, the judge overruled him stating that the coroner had clearly warned the prisoner at the inquest that anything she might say could be used against her.

Inspector Raymond continued by saying that the prisoner had complained of not being allowed bail and he had replied, "How could you expect it in a case like this? You are charged with poisoning your husband." The prisoner had then replied that no person could prove that she had poisoned him. He had then informed her that she had told the coroner that she had been in Walsall with Hannah Mason and that the police would trace where the poison was purchased to which she replied that she had never been to a druggists in her life or purchased poison. She had only been in Walsall to purchase items for her daughter.

The final witness was Mr. Chevasse who repeated the post mortem results. Once again he stressed the quantity of arsenic found in the victim's stomach and went into great detail concerning the tests done to reveal if it was indeed arsenic and the amount discovered. Further tests were carried out at Birmingham under Messrs. Southwell, "the most eminent analytical chemists".

Mr. Yardley for the Defence argued that the tests applied could not be adequately relied on to indicate the presence of arsenic, but Mr. Chevasse was adamant that they could. When asked by Mr. Yardley if arsenic might be absorbed into a body externally (the powder being rubbed in to cure the itch) Mr. Chevasse agreed that it could be, but "not to the extent that was present in the deceased's body". As to the "itch" he said that he could find no marks on the corpse to suggest that disease.

All witnesses heard the judge asked if the defendant had made a statement at the inquest. That was then read out by Mr. Bellamy, junior, the Clerk of the Arraigns. The gist of the lengthy statement was that Sarah denied ever having purchased poison in her life or having had any in the house. She and her husband had never had any quarrels concerning Phillips and that it was only when Hannah Smith, her husband's sister, had rumoured that he had been poisoned that anything amiss was mentioned. She herself had been to Doctor Goodall and asked him to examine the body, but when she told him that

Mr. Chevasse had been to look at the body he had refused.

All the evidence heard Mr. Yardley addressed the jury. He argued that his client could not possibly have mixed such a quantity of arsenic (half an ounce) with butter without it being obvious in the gruel or without it being tasted. He also argued that if she had poisoned her husband then she would have tried to keep it secret, but she did want to call for a doctor and the neighbours were allowed into the bedroom. As to the speed of trying to obtain a death certificate he argued that it was the custom "of persons in the class of the prisoner to bury their dead on a Sunday" and that was her only reason for wishing a quick funeral. Finally, as to the supposed relationship with Phillips he argued that several close friends had testified that they knew nothing of it, including Charles Westwood, her son.

Having summed up all the evidence the judge told the jury not to be swayed by the fact that it was "an unfortunate woman at the bar", but to judge the case on the evidence only. That done they retired and after only a quarter of an hour they returned a verdict of "Guilty", but with a recommendation for mercy. However, when asked by the judge on what grounds they made that recommendation they could give no reasonable answer and so he denied their plea.

The general noise of the court having been subdued, the judge then passed the death sentence on Sarah. Mr. Bellamy, then asked Sarah if she had anything to say. At that point she trembled violently and appeared to be about to faint, but finally managed to blurt out that she was pregnant. (Though it would not save her from execution it would delay it until after the birth.)

Immediately the court was cleared and the doors closed. A jury of married women was formed from those present and Sarah was taken into the jury room to be examined. After about three quarters of an hour the women returned to the courtroom and Sarah was replaced into the chair in the dock. Having been asked about her state, the women announced that she was not pregnant and Sarah was taken from the room. She was so ill that she had to be carried down the steps.

Her stay in prison was short. She had few visitors. Her parents, Charles Parker and his wife, had long since given up on their daughter and refused to visit. They clearly thought that she had disgraced the family. The Parkers had lived in Chorley and Sarah had been born in 1802. Part of the labouring class they had bettered themselves by hard work and had managed to buy a small piece of copyhold land in 1817 on the outskirts of Burntwood, near Longdon, on which they had built a cottage where they still

lived. By 1843 their property had increased considerably, then owning five fields along with their house, garden and outhouses. However, at an early age Sarah had acquired a loose reputation and had had an illegitimate child about eighteen months before her marriage to John Westwood (not his). It was then that they had disowned her.

On Tuesday, January 9th she had received a visit from Hannah Smith, a sister of her late husband, and she was accompanied by a man

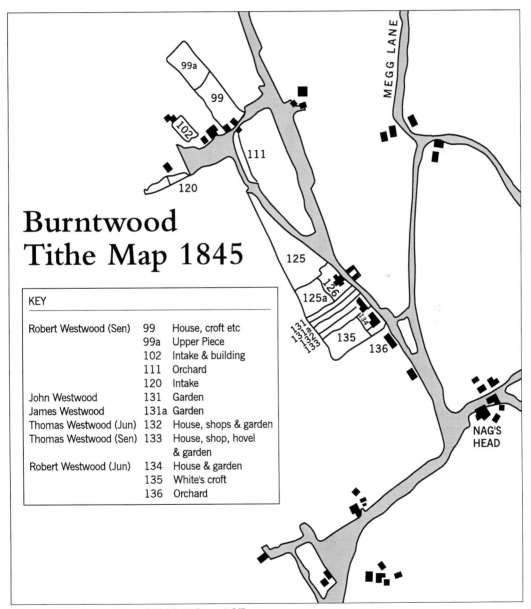

Map 4. By kind permission of Lichfield Record Office.

who claimed to be her brother. However, the guards were suspicious and under interrogation by the governor it transpired that the man was none other than Phillips whom Sarah had expressed a wish to see. He was not permitted the visit and instantly ordered from the prison.

On Thursday January 11th two of her children, Charles and Harriett, visited half expecting that their mother might have received a letter deferring her death sentence to one of life imprisonment. When they realised that she had not they both became very depressed. Later reports had it that both children were sure that their father had committed suicide. Harriett was reported as having said that she had overheard her father threaten to kill himself on the Saturday before the tragedy. In the final moments of the visit Sarah begged Charles to look after the family and his father's shop.

On the morning of the execution (Saturday, January 13th) Sarah was so weak that she had to be carried to the gallows and placed on a stool under the rope where she sat until the bell tolled eight o'clock, the traditional execution time. Her last words as the rope was placed around her neck were, "It's hard to die for a thing one's innocent of." The trapdoor opened and she breathed her last.

Footnote:- It seems from the 1845 Tithe Map that Sarah's wish that her son, Charles, should keep the family business going and look after the family did not happen as the register of property owners or lessees has no mention of him. It would seem that the nailer's shop was taken over by one of John's brothers, probably Thomas, and the children cared for by him.

That is probably born out by the fact that Christ Church's Parish Register records Mary Westwood (22) marrying James Davies, a 28 year old miner from Burntwood, on June 18th, 1845 with Thomas Westwood being registered as her father. However, just to confuse those tracing their family tree there was also a Mary Ann Westwood who married a nailer, Henry Phillips, on August 31st, 1845; her father being Robert Westwood.

Charles Westwood, while still a minor, married one Maria Westwood on September 13th, 1846. Just to confuse matters further Maria's father was a Robert Westwood, a nailer. Had Charles married his first cousin or was that a different Westwood family? Incidentally Charles was still working as a nailer.

Finally Eliza married George Mitchell, a labourer, on October 5th, 1852.

THE LESSER OF THREE EVILS
Cannock 1894

Readers may have wondered why, when a criminal goes to court having committed more than one crime, the Authorities prefer to try them for one offence only. The reason quite simply is that they always act on the crime that is almost a certainty to obtain a conviction. If they take a chance and go for everything and the criminal is found not guilty for some of the crimes that may affect the jury's perception on the otherwise foolproof case. That was the case in 1894 when three men were charged with attacking an old lady.

Just after seven o'clock in the morning on Sunday April 22nd Arthur Walker and Thomas Richardson, both of Bridgtown, decided to take a stroll into Cannock. They arrived there at 7.20 a.m. by St. Luke's Church clock and then continued their walk down Hatherton Lane. Thomas, because of a call of nature, stopped to relieve himself and while doing so noticed something dreadful in the nearby field. Calling to Arthur the pair went to investigate and discovered the body of a woman in a distressed state, though she was not quite dead. They immediately went for the police.

Sergeant Gibbs and Constable Jackson arrived shortly and realising the seriousness of the situation sent for Dr. Butter, the police surgeon, who dispatched a stretcher with Walker and an officer while he followed on behind. When he arrived the woman had been placed on the stretcher and he then examined her. Certain that she was in a dying state he ordered that she be taken to the workhouse where she unfortunately died a few hours later.

The police began their investigations into the woman's movements the previous day. They were helped in the fact that they knew the victim well because of her "very drunken habits". She was Elsie Cotterill who lived with relatives in Longford Lane, Hatherton.

By the evening they had arrested Fredrick Holford, a miner from Four Crosses and shortly after two other men were detained at Shareshill. They were George Hassall and George Winfield, both banksmen from Calf Heath. All three were taken before Mr. Gilpin, the magistrate, on the Monday and remanded until after the inquest.

That inquest began before Mr. Morgan on the afternoon of Tuesday April 24th at the Boardroom, Union Workhouse. The jury having viewed the body the first witness was called. William Baker, a boat loader from Hatherton, said that the deceased was sixty eight year old Elsie Cotterill, a cousin to his wife, and she had lived with them since the death of her husband. She had no means of support and so he and his wife had kept her without payment for the last twelve months. She had two other relatives – a brother in Cannock Workhouse and a sister in the Potteries. He had last seen her alive on the Saturday when he was in his garden. She was dressed up and said that she was going into Cannock for some tobacco and asked him for a handful of gillies (wallflowers) which he gave her. She was very cheerful and said that she should not be long away.

He had to admit to the hearing that she was "a woman of fearful drunken habits" and, despite being warned by the doctor to stop drinking, had been worse than ever for the last six months. Occasionally she had borrowed two or three coppers from him or his wife to go to Cannock, but had usually come back "helplessly drunk". She had taken to staying out nights on occasion and he had even warned her that if she did not mend her ways he might turn her out. On the night in question his wife sat up until one o'clock in the morning waiting for her to come home, but thought nothing of it when she did not arrive as she had stayed out many times.

In her defence William stated that apart from the drink she had always been "morally right", an important statement in view of the evidence to come.

Robert Grigg, landlord of the Royal Oak Inn, Cannock, was next to take the stand. He said that he had noticed the deceased at seven o'clock in the evening in Market Place and just before ten o'clock she had entered his inn. She was already a little the worse for drink and so he refused to serve her with any more. Then Holford, one of the accused, ordered a glass of hot whiskey and water and gave it to Elsie. Mrs. Grigg had served him, but when the witness found out he snatched it from the deceased and put it away. He then told Mrs. Cotterill to go and she left in the company of Holford. That would be about ten o'clock and he last saw the pair walking across the top of the Bowling Green in the direction of Hatherton.

Questioned about Elsie's time at the inn Grigg said that she was only there about eight to ten minutes. He noticed that she carried a basket, newspapers and what he believed was a broccoli.

Holford had bought a sixpenny worth of rum in a split soda bottle and had tried to give the deceased some of it, but he prevented that from happening.

After further questions from the jury Grigg said that he had known Elsie for about twelve months and knew of her drunken habits, though he had never seen her drinking with men before. As to the other two accused he said that he could not swear to seeing them at his inn on the night.

It was then the turn of Thomas Richardson, a hairdresser, to give his evidence. He stated that he and Arthur Walker were going along Hatherton Lane on the Sunday morning at about 7.30 and when they got down to the field opposite the "Sitch" and passing the gate he saw something lying about 10 or 12 yards into the field near to the hedge. The gate was about 18 inches open and so he asked Arthur to go and see what the object was. When he was within two yards of the object Arthur exclaimed, "It's a woman and her face is knocked all to pieces." He then told the hearing that he had never seen such a sight – "it was like a malkin".

*Although there are many definitions of "malkin" the one that the witness probably

18. The Royal Oak, Cannock c.1900

meant was a scarecrow, a ragged puppet or grotesque effigy, though he could have meant a female spectre or demon.

*A sitch is usually a gully or hollow or can be a ditch or channel through which a tiny stream flows, often dried up in summer. Here it was the local nickname for the field.

Thomas continued his description of the scene. He said that the woman was lying on her back with her clothes thrown up. When he asked Arthur if she were alive he said she was as her legs were twitching. Arthur had shouted at the woman to get up, but she did not move. It was then that they decided to fetch the police. He returned to the scene with Sergeant Gibbs and Constable Jackson, leaving Arthur at the station. When they arrived back at the scene the woman had not moved at all.

Arthur Walker, a miner from Bridgtown, corroborated the evidence given by Thomas adding a few more details. He said that he picked up half an ounce of tobacco lying near to where the victim was lying and he noticed a lot of footmarks nearby as though there had been a bit of a struggle. Also there was a little blood on the side of the woman's face. He and Constable Jackson went for Dr. Butter and he helped to carry the stretcher back to the scene.

Miss Lizzie West, a nurse at the Cannock Workhouse, Wolverhampton Road, said that she took charge of Elsie Cotterill when she was brought to the home at 8.55 on the Sunday morning. At the time she was alive, but unconscious and never regained consciousness, dying at ten minutes to twelve. Unfortunately that meant that no "dying declaration" had been made.

The final witness was Dr. John Kerr Butter who stated that he gave the deceased a full examination when she arrived at the workhouse. She was unconscious and the pupils were insensitive to light. There was dried blood in her nostrils and around the mouth and right cheek and saliva and blood about her hair and neck. There was a small abrasion on both knees and her right hand was blood stained. There were bruises on the right wrist and the forearm and on the inside of the arm above the elbow. The outer clothing was disarranged and muddy in places. He diagnosed that she was suffering from apoplexy at the time of admission to the

workhouse. (Apoplexy is an illness which hinders voluntary movement and awareness - a type of fit.)

19. Dr. Butter in uniform c.1900.

After Elsie's death the doctor carried out a post mortem assisted by Dr. Riley, the workhouse medical officer. They discovered further bruising to the left hip and several to the head. On examining the brain he found a blood clot on the right side though the left side was healthy. The lungs were found to be congested and the heart showed early signs of disease. The liver was contracted and "nob-nailed", what was known as "gin drinker's liver", obviously brought about by her heavy drinking over the years. Apart from a slightly congested stomach the remainder of her body was healthy.

Closer examination revealed that Elsie had been "outraged", as the Victorians preferred to call indecent assault or rape, and roughly used. During such an attack she was likely to rupture a blood vessel with the organs as they were and the extra exertion in trying to prevent such an attack or struggle would induce apoplexy. In his estimation it was the apoplexy which caused the death.

The coroner and jury wanted to know precisely what had caused the death because that would lead to the exact charges against the prisoners. Under questioning Dr. Butter said that the attack would produce apoplexy, but a mere fall due to her half drunken state could have produced it. In other words had she fallen before the attack had taken place that might have brought on apoplexy. The deceased might then have become partially stupefied and in that state might have been outraged without being able to struggle.

As that point was crucial to the charges the doctor was questioned in more detail. He said that the ground where the body was found seemed to have evidence of a struggle and the bruises on her arms might suggest a struggle. However, those bruises could have been made by persons trying to carry the victim as she was a very heavy woman. He could not say definitely that death was caused or accelerated by a struggle, but it might have been. It was quite possible for apoplexy to come on naturally due to the state of the deceased's organs.

Strangely he finished by adding that the bruise on the knee had the appearance of being caused by a finger nail as though she had been held down, but the blood from the nose could have been caused by a slight blow when carrying the woman.

It was that lack of definite proof of actual death which then led the coroner to close the inquest in the hope that further investigations by the police might produce clearer evidence as to the events of that tragic evening.

The adjourned inquest began on May 1st. A large crowd had lined the Wolverhampton Road between the Police Station and the Union Workhouse to catch a glimpse of the three accused men as they were escorted to the hearing. The men were represented by Mr. Gillespie while Superintendent Barrett conducted the case for the police.

Sergeant Gibbs was the first to be called. He said that at about 7.40 a.m. on Sunday April 22nd Mr. Walker and Mr. Richardson had told him of the body in Hatherton Lane. He and Constable Jackson went there immediately and found the woman lying about 18 yards inside the field known locally as "Sitch Field". Her body was about three feet from the ditch with her head towards it. He recognised her as Elsie

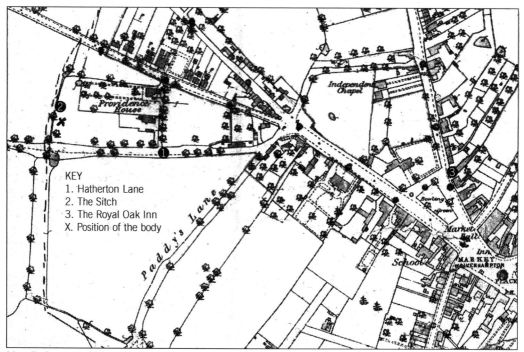

KEY
1. Hatherton Lane
2. The Sitch
3. The Royal Oak Inn
X. Position of the body

Map 5. Cannock 1884 showing Hatherton Lane.

Cotterill, a widow from Longford Lane. Her face had dried blood on it and saliva ran down to the back of her neck and bonnet. Her clothes were turned up and her dress and bonnet torn, the feathers of which were broken. There were marks of a struggle.

From information given he arrested twenty three year old Frederick Holford at 5.00 p.m. at his home, Watling Street, Four Crosses, Hatherton, and charged him on suspicion of causing the death of the deceased. Once cautioned the prisoner said, "I was in the Oak with her. We came out and went up the road together. When by the shop at the top of the road two men came up to us and one said, "It's my aunt. We will take her home." I left them with her and came straight home with Winfield and Hassall who live at Calf Heath." While he took the prisoner to the station Constable Jackson searched the house and Mrs. Holford produced a pair of trousers which the prisoner had worn on the night in question.

After arresting Holford the witness went to Shareshill Church where at about 7.45 p.m. he arrested twenty one year old George Winfield as he was leaving the church. When he was cautioned he said, "I will tell you the truth, sir. I and Hassall came up in front of the woman and Holford and the other two, whom I don't know, were sitting by Evans' blacksmith's shop, one on one side of the road and the other on the other side. I and Hassall went in front to the end of Gorsey Lane, waited a bit and then went back to the brook on the nearer side to Cannock. The woman was lying down and Holford and the two men were standing by her. One of those two men said, "Let's carry her into the field," and all five of us did. It was then that four of us outraged her, but not Hassall.

When questioned as to how he knew the deceased Sergeant Gibbs said that he had previously seen her around Cannock during the last four months. She had been brought to the station once by Constable Gunn when she was drunk and she had to be escorted home. As to her character he had heard no complaints save for her being "fond of her half pints".

Constable Jackson corroborated the evidence of the sergeant and added that he had arrested nineteen year old George Hassall also in Shareshill Churchyard. After charging and cautioning him Hassall said, "I went down the lane with George Winfield in front of Fred Holford and the woman. We heard them stop and so turned back. The woman was lying by the side of the road and Holford and two other men were standing nearby. One of the "strange" men said, "Let's carry her into the field," and we did. I did not touch her after we had let her down. We left the two strangers with her."

Also questioned about his knowledge of the deceased the constable said that he had been in the area for about four years and had seen the deceased drunk several times. However, like the sergeant, he too knew nothing against her moral character.

The final witness was Daniel Moore, a gas fitter living in Hatherton Lane. He said that at about 10.30 p.m. he was putting up a shed in his garden and saw the deceased in the lane with a man. Both were on the footpath and he thought the man was taking the woman home as she seemed to have had some beer. He also saw two men going down the middle of the lane after the man and woman. He heard the woman say, "It's my uncle; it's my uncle. Take me home." He heard nothing after.

20. Len Belcher in Hatherton Lane.

Mr. Adams, the foreman of the jury, asked him about the two men, but Daniel said that he did not recognise either of them. As to where the body was found he said that it was 200 to 300 yards from his house.

When the coroner began his summation of the evidence he started by asking Superintendent Barratt about the two strangers in the lane and Barratt had to admit that they had been unable to trace either man. Turning to the jury he said that the medical evidence was clear - the woman had died from apoplexy. However, they had to decide "whether that came on naturally or whether it was produced by the unlawful act of any person or persons. If they decided on the second course then those persons would be responsible for the murder or manslaughter of the woman."

The coroner then went carefully through Dr. Butter's statement showing how the doctor could not be certain as to what had caused the apoplexy. As to the signs of a struggle he said that with "five persons carrying a heavy woman over the grass there would be a good deal of tramping about". As for the bruises suffered by the deceased there could be two interpretations - either she was forcibly held down or they were caused by men in a half drunken state carrying her. The blood on the face and torn clothes would come in the same category. There was no doubt as to the outrage, the prisoners had confessed to that, but did that outrage cause or accelerate the apoplexy. If so they should return a verdict of murder or manslaughter. As for the prisoner Hassall, who had not taken part in the outrage, just by standing by and not trying to stop it he was aiding and abetting and therefore in law equally liable.

The jury wanted to consider their verdict in private and so the court was cleared. After about fifteen minutes they announced they were ready. Their verdict - the deceased died from apoplexy. Like the doctor they had refused to be drawn on the precise cause of death.

There was, however, another chance for justice for the unfortunate Elsie Cotterill. What would the magistrates' court decide? That hearing began on Monday May 7th at Penkridge Police Court before Lord Hatherton, Mr. Gilpin and

Mr. Chetwynd. Exactly why the case was moved to Penkridge was not made clear; perhaps to avoid emotion and allow cool reasoning to take precedence. Whatever the reason the Prosecution, led by Mr. Hand, began by stating that they would not be prosecuting on the graver charge of murder or manslaughter. Instead they would argue against Holford for the case of rape and against the others for aiding and abetting. Clearly the Prosecution had decided that the graver charge was almost impossible to prove and so had gone for the more certain conviction in the hope that the Bench would send the men to the Assize Court, with the possible exception of Hassall.

Most witnesses called were those at the coroner's court, but there were several new ones. Frederick Bennett, a labourer from Hatherton, said that he went to the Royal Oak in Cannock at about 8.30 on the fatal night and he noticed all three prisoners there. He left at about nine o'clock and they were still there, but when he returned at about half past ten they had all gone. When he left at eleven o'clock he walked home over Shoal Hill. Asked how he could be sure it was the three men Frederick said that he had had a glass of beer with Hassall and Winfield and Holford was with them.

Arthur Lindop, a carter living at Hatherton, stated that on that evening he was returning home from Cannock at about 10.30 p.m. by the Sitch when he saw three men standing up and one man, as he thought, lying down. The one on the ground was groaning. The witness remarked to the men, "He's in rum form, isn't he, mate?" and one of the men replied, "Go on, he's all right, or you'll get one," (meaning we will thump you).

When asked exactly where the incident had taken place Arthur said it was beside the road, about 300 yards from Daniel Moore's house and close to the field where the deceased was found. The three men he saw were within 60 yards of the gate to the field in question, on the Cannock side of the brook bridge. As to the men he did not recognise any of them.

Sergeant Gibbs took the stand again and then produced the clothes worn by Holford on the night of April 21st. There was mud on the brim and band of the hat, a woman's hair on the waistcoat and dirt on the coat cuff. He had also compared Holford's boots with the prints on the sods of earth taken from the ditch near to where the body was found. They corresponded exactly with the left boot. There were prints of a right boot in the ditch, but they were partly covered with water.

All the evidence heard the prisoners were committed for trial at the next Assizes. Mr. Craddock for the Defence applied for bail for Hassall, but the Bench said they could not make any difference between the men and so refused it.

The case came before Mr. Justice Hawkins at the Assize Court in Stafford on Wednesday July 25th, 1894. All three were charged with the manslaughter of Elsie Cotterill and also charged with rape and indecent assault. They pleaded guilty to the latter charge and not guilty to the others.

Mr. Jelf, Q.C., representing the Prosecution began by saying that, having read all the depositions of the witnesses and the accused, he felt that the charge of indecent assault, with the judge's sanction, seemed to meet the justice of the case. The medical evidence showed that the deceased died from apoplexy, but there was evidence to show there had been an indecent attack on her by the three men. However, considering the difficulties in proving the graver charges of manslaughter and rape he hoped the Crown would be satisfied with an acquittal on those charges.

Mr. Herbert for the Defence stated that he had carefully considered the evidence and had advised his clients that there was no chance of escaping the charge of indecent assault. However, with respect to Hassall he asked his lordship to make some distinction as it appeared from the statements that, although he was present, he took no part in the assault. As for the sentence for indecent assault he hoped the judge would take into consideration the fact that the men had already been in prison for three months.

The judge in his summing up fully agreed with the Prosecution, adding "the difficulties in the way of obtaining a conviction or asking the jury to convict the prisoners of manslaughter were insurmountable". He failed to see how a conviction could be obtained considering the medical evidence. He, therefore, would proceed to pass sentence on the charge of indecent assault only.

Having deliberated over night Mr. Justice Hawkins decided that Hassall should be given a sentence of three months hard labour while Winfield and Holford should each get four months. There was no mention of their previous three months in gaol awaiting the trial, but it was most likely that that time would be taken off the sentence. If that was the case George Hassall would have walked free after the trial.

Had the men got off lightly? Even with today's advances in forensic science murder would be difficult to prove, but the charge of manslaughter would be possible. The charge of rape, with modern D.N.A. techniques, would also be highly likely to succeed.

A CHRISTMAS NIGHTMARE
Chadsmoor 1881

Christmas - the season of goodwill to all men - yet strangely and rather sadly the time of year when the largest percentage of marriages break down. In fact divorce solicitors and lawyers recognise the first week of January to be their busiest time. Psychologists lay the blame on families, already under marital stress, suddenly being "forced" together in their homes for days without any possibility of escape. Unfortunately, as we all know, it is the children who suffer most in those situations, some in danger of physical harm. Was it just such a tragic situation which led to the untimely death of eight weeks old Hannah Parker?

Amelia Catherine Parker had being courting Joseph Holden, a miner, for some time when she suddenly found herself pregnant. Because of the possible social stigma, Victorian England was very prudish about such affairs, the two were quite possibly forced into a marriage which neither really wanted. Joseph was the more upset and tried to relieve his frustration by drinking, but eventually the two were married on December 4th, 1881, five weeks after the child was born. Could his frustration have led to Joseph's resentment of the child? Whatever might have been the case it was to have dreadful consequences.

On Christmas Eve Joseph was out drinking again and at nine o'clock returned home to find his wife and child in the house. Worried about his possible behaviour Amelia and Clara Stokes, a relative, managed to get him upstairs to bed. However, he refused to stay there and came down again. What happened next was sudden - he simply grabbed hold of the child and held it tightly to his chest. When Amelia managed to prize the baby from him the child was already dead. Realising what had happened Joseph ran

from the house saying that he would end his own life. The police finally tracked him down hiding in a nearby shed.

Conscious of the raw emotions created by the possible murder of a child the police and coroner tried to keep the time and place of the inquest secret, but the news leaked out and there was "considerable excitement manifested in the neighbourhood" as the time drew near. On the afternoon of Tuesday December 27th an "excited crowd" gathered outside the Anglesey Hotel, Hednesford. Inside Mr. Morgan, the coroner, did his best to control the hearing.

Fifty four year old Caroline Parker, grandmother of the child, was the first to give evidence. She told the hearing that her daughter, Amelia, and Joseph Holden lived with her at Holly Cottage, West Chadsmoor. He had lodged with them for about eighteen months after he started courting her daughter. Around six thirty on the evening of December 24th she arrived home from Hednesford and found her daughter, the girl Clara Stokes and the child in the house. The witness fed the child and left the house again to go to Hednesford Market. When she got back at around ten o'clock her daughter was standing against the wall and Holden was on the floor with the child, apparently dead, on his lap. Amelia simply said, "O mother, he's done it; he's killed my child."

Caroline then said that she took the child from him and untied its clothes and held it to the fire to attempt to revive it because she believed that it was dead. However, it was quite lifeless and did not recover. Blood came from the nose and mouth. Then she grabbed Holden by the hair saying, "You villain, what did you do this for?" He replied, "You can pull all the hair off my head, but I have not done it." He then raised

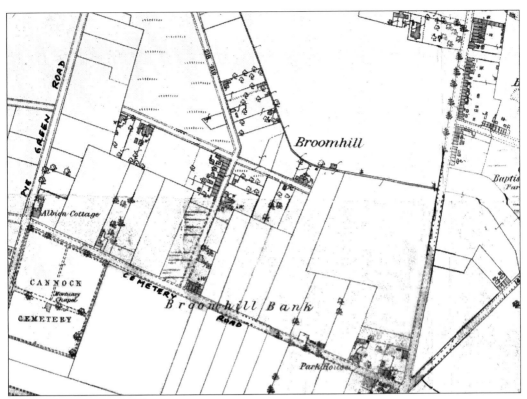

Map 6. West Chadsmoor 1884.

himself up from the fireplace and said, "I must go and give myself up to the police. I may as well die now as at any other time."

At that the witness ordered him out of the house, but he replied, "If I go out of the house she (his wife) will have to go." On being told that she would not go he asked for his jacket and after getting it he went into the parlour, took his knife out of his pocket, sharpened it on the step and said that he would kill himself.

When questioned by the coroner Caroline said that she did not think Holden was sober at the time. He had on more than one occasion threatened to kill the child and she had taken the baby to her own bed one night because she feared for its safety. She also admitted that her daughter had had another child previous to the deceased child though she did not say who the father had been or what had happened to that baby. However, she insisted that her daughter and Holden "seemed comfortable together".

As to the fits that her daughter suffered Caroline said that they "came on at irregular intervals and were sometimes very severe" and that they "came on quite suddenly". They had not improved after childbirth.

Twenty two year old Amelia was next to take the stand, but she was very shaken and appeared dazed by the situation. She said that her husband had arrived home at about nine o'clock on the night and appeared sober, although he had been drinking. She and Clara Stokes put him to bed, but he came straight back down. He began to threaten her and so she left the house, but he followed her and pulled her back into the room. She then sat down and gave the baby its feed at the breast and he sat down on the floor beside her. Without saying anything he got up, snatched the child from her, taking hold of it by the head and feet. She took the child from him when it appeared to be dead, but he snatched it back again. When her mother arrived back she told her what he had done, but he denied it.

When questioned she said that he had threatened to kill her and the child only three weeks ago. Then he had caught hold of the witness by the throat.

As was his right in law Joseph Holden was

allowed to question the witness himself. He suggested to his wife that she had had a fit on the fatal night and had smothered the baby during it. However, its was very evident to the court from the answers she gave that her memory was "faulty" and the dreadful series of events had completely unsettled her mind.

If Amelia was somewhat dazed by the proceedings her niece, thirteen year old Clara Stokes, was more confident in her evidence. She testified that she was in the house at Chadsmoor on Christmas Eve when Holden arrived back and he was not sober. He asked her to give him a razor and when she said that she could not find one he replied, "I will wring your ---- neck if you don't find me one." She was then so frightened that she ran out of the house to find a neighbour.

When she got back Holden was sitting on the floor. He asked his wife where his sisters and brothers were and when she said that she did not know he replied, "If you do not tell me I will --- well strangle you." He tried to grab Mrs. Holden by the neck, but she threw her head back. He then seized the child and held it by the throat for three or four minutes and immediately after he began to cry. The child closed its eyes and its head fell back, but it never cried. Mrs. Holden said, "You've done it now, Joe. It's gone; it's gone," to which he replied, "Has it? I shall say I did not do it."

Clara continued by saying that she then heard footsteps outside and ran from the house. There she met Mrs. Parker and her own father.

When asked by the coroner about Holden's previous behaviour she said that three weeks previously she had heard him threaten his wife and the child. He had had an open razor in his hands and had said, "I'll kill the young - --." As to Mrs. Holden having fits she said that she was "subject to them", but was sure that she did not have one on the night in question. The room was lit with a candle and she would have been able to see clearly if a fit had taken place.

Sergeant Whalley stationed at Hednesford testified that on the Saturday night at a quarter to eleven he had been informed by a man named Ward about the tragedy. He arrived at Mrs. Parker's at eleven and saw the dead child lying on Mrs. Ward's knee. It was bleeding from the nose.

He then went in search of Holden and about ten minutes later found him in a wooden shed not far from the house. He was concealed under some straw and when the witness removed it he appeared to be asleep. He then asked the man his name to which the defendant replied, "Wright." He still maintained that that was his name when asked a second time. At that the sergeant took the man outside and a neighbour identified him as Holden.

Once arrested and handcuffed the defendant said, "Well, I have only got once to die." He was not charged at that time, only cautioned and taken to Hednesford Police Station. On the way the defendant said, "It will be a nice thing if I have my neck stretched for that which I have not done." After that a constable continued with the defendant to the station while the witness returned to the house. Once there he obtained the deceased's night-gown which was stained with blood. (That had been produced as evidence to the court.)

21. Who is the policeman standing with the miners?

At about four o'clock the next morning when the defendant was sober the witness charged Holden with causing the death of his infant child. In his defence he replied, "I did not do it. It was dead when I took it from my wife and I sat down on the hearth with it."

Mr. M. Taylor, surgeon, said that he had carried out the post mortem on the Tuesday morning and externally the child was well nourished and well developed for a two month old baby. Internally the brain was congested with blood, though in itself it was healthy, and the right cavities of the heart were also congested with blood. The lungs were also congested, especially the left one. The rest of the organs were perfectly healthy and normal. In his opinion those symptoms were consistent with strangulation and he was sure death was caused by that method. There might not have been any great pressure, but in a child of only eight weeks a slight continued pressure which caused stoppage of air to the lungs would soon cause death.

The coroner also questioned the surgeon about Mrs. Holden's mental condition to which the doctor said that "epileptic attacks, such as she was used to, would tend to weaken the intellect and cause an amount of mental imbecility". *Remember anything slightly unusual in behaviour in Victorian times was frequently labelled as imbecility as they had little knowledge of mental conditions. Their frequent method of dealing with such persons was to lock them up in lunatic asylums.

The final witness was Mr. G. Elliot, a Hednesford doctor, who stated that he had been called to the house in Chadsmoor at about twelve o'clock on the fatal evening. On making an external examination he found a slight discoloration of the skin under the left ear and some bloody froth around the nose and mouth. When he turned the body over more blood came from both mouth and nose. On the Tuesday he had helped Mr. Taylor with the post mortem and agreed with his findings.

The coroner in his summing up drew the jury's attention to Mrs. Holden saying that he could not help but think that her memory was affected by the fits she had, but the evidence given by Clara Stokes had been given in "an excellent manner". He also reminded them that drunkenness was not an excuse for crime and that there did not seem to have been any provocation for the supposed attack by the defendant. Finally, he stated that if they thought death was caused by strangulation then "however painful it might be it was their duty to return a verdict of Wilful Murder".

Before they retired the jury heard a statement from twenty four year old Joseph Holden who insisted that he had not committed the crime. However, it took them only minutes to decide that he was guilty of the wilful murder of his own child and should stand trial at the next Assizes.

22. Hednesford Police Station, Cannock Road c.1970. The station was first opened in 1878.

Unlike today the press were given free access to view any criminal and the following appeared in the *Cannock Advertiser:- His conduct has been somewhat singular* (while in Hednesford Police Station). *At times he appears to be fainty, then he commences to walk round the cell. At others he sits with his face buried in his hands; occasionally he bursts out crying, but soon commences to sing hymns.* Then quite ironically the reporter adds - *He is said to be a fair singer.*

On Friday December 30th Holden was taken before Mr. Gilpin, the magistrate. Evidence was given of threats he had used at work and elsewhere, though unfortunately the newspaper of the day did not detail any of them. When he had nothing to say in his defence he was once again committed to trial at the next Assizes.

On Wednesday January 22nd, 1882 Joseph Holden was tried for the murder of his baby daughter before Mr. Justice North at Stafford Assizes. There were several witnesses who had not been present at the inquest, but had appeared before the magistrates. Thomas Merrick, a miner and neighbour of Mrs. Parker, said that he had gone to the house after the commotion to help, but it was too late. He remembered Holden threatening to "knock the child's brains out" on one occasion before when he, the defendant, was drunk. Likewise Edward Haycock, a workmate of the prisoner, said that about a fortnight before Christmas Holden told him that the baby had kept him awake all night and he "had a mind to knock its brains out".

All the other witnesses having given the same evidence as at the coroner's inquest Mr. Plowden for the Defence began his summing up. He argued that it could have easily been Mrs. Holden who killed the child in one of her fits, but because all of her relations accused her husband and supported her at the time of the tragedy she then accused her husband of the murder without knowing exactly what had happened. Even if he was guilty of the homicide of the child his intentions were not to kill it – his actions were not premeditated. Surely it was not the actions of a murderer to sit at the hearth and nurse the baby which he had just killed? At the most the jury should find him guilty of manslaughter and not murder.

Mr. Plowden's argument seemed to have swayed the jury somewhat because they did find Joseph Holden guilty of Manslaughter. The judge seemed surprised and deferred the sentence until the next day. When passing sentence he commented that "the jury had taken a merciful consideration of his case and he ought to be very thankful that he (the judge) had not now to pass sentence of death. As it was he must pass a very severe sentence which would be one of twenty years penal servitude."

BULLETS NEVER SETTLE ARGUMENTS
Cheslyn Hay 1870 - 1885

Thankfully laws have been passed today which prevent the ordinary person from carrying a gun, but for the villagers of Cheslyn Hay in the 1870's and 80's it must have felt that they had suddenly been visited by the Wild West of America. While most men were satisfied to settle their differences with a fist fight on the common or in the back yard, some took it into their mind to end a dispute with a gun. What follows are three episodes, two remarkably at the same pit, where usually peace loving citizens suddenly became gunslingers.

John Farnell who lived in Town Well Road was head engineer at the Wyrley and Cannock Colliery Company and had seen fit to take under his wing James Allsopp, a young lad from Essington Wood who was of "irregular habits" (probably drink which led to lack of wanting to work). John treated him like a son and despite James appearing at work late on many occasions and not properly attending the engine which was his job, John had forgiven the lad and had even reinstated him several times. Although a big man John Farnell had always remained even tempered when dealing with the infuriating lad, but on the evening of September 16th, 1870 something snapped.

As the buzzer went at six o'clock on the Friday evening for the change of shift John's son, Samuel, left his post at the engine, but James had not arrived to take over. It was not until half past six that James sauntered towards the blacksmith's shop only to be confronted by John. When questioned as to his late arrival James must have said something quite abusive because the big man suddenly slapped him across the face. James, although considerably smaller, kicked John in the shins, but was then hit again by John which knocked him to the ground. For a few seconds all was quiet, but then James got up, drew a pistol and fired at John hitting him just above the liver.

Realising what he had done, James ran off for a few yards, threatening workers as he went, but then calmly began to walk towards the canal. Although injured John managed to walk to get help, clutching his side which was bleeding badly. In the meantime men had raced to fetch the colliery manager who then sent for the police. It was Constable Lindop who finally caught up with James at Broadlanes, near Essington. However, before he could arrest him James fired at the constable, narrowly missing his body, but hitting his coat. After a struggle James was arrested and taken to Cannock Police Station where he was charged with wounding John Farnell with intent to do bodily harm. Unfortunately John died the following morning and the charge immediately changed to that of murder.

The inquest began on Monday September 19th at the Red Lion Inn, Wyrley Bank before Mr. W. H. Phillips, the Deputy Coroner of Staffordshire. Mr. Brinsley, the managing director of the Company, identified the body and stated that James Allsopp had been with the Company for two years, lately as an engine tenter. He was under the supervision of the deceased who had in fact given him the job. On the Saturday, when John Farnell gave his dying statement, the deceased had pointed out the prisoner as the man who had fired at him and injured him.

*Victorians placed great emphasis on dying statements believing them to be the absolute truth. The idea of lying to gain revenge never entered their minds. In some cases the lack of a dying statement actually got the accused off the charge, especially when there was no other witness to the crime other than the perpetrator.

23. The Red Lion, Wyrley Bank in 1914.

On occasions, as with this case, the accused was actually present when the statement was made.

That dying statement, made before Mr. Gilpin, a local magistrate; Superintendent Holland; Mr. Brinsley; Mr. Taylor, the doctor; and James Allsop, was read out in court. It stated, "About six o'clock on the evening of the 16th I was waiting for James Allsopp to come on night duty. He arrived about half past six and I asked him why he did not come at the proper time, stating that I would have to discharge him. Allsopp was saucy and I struck him with my open hand. Allsopp took a running kick at me and I struck him with a clenched fist. Allsopp then started off and when about two or three yards from me he fired a pistol at me and the contents of the pistol struck me in the left side and I fell bleeding." Throughout the making of the statement, according to Mr. Taylor, Allsopp showed no emotion.

Mr. Taylor was the next witness. He stated that he had been called to John Farnell's home to examine the wound on the Friday evening and found that the man was very exhausted from the loss of a great deal of blood. Some missile had penetrated Farnell's thickly lined pilot coat and shirt and had entered the body immediately over the liver. In an attempt to remove the missile a probe was passed into the wound some three inches, but could not dislodge it. Mr. V. Jackson, a surgeon from Wolverhampton, was also present and he remarked that "it was a hopeless case" and expected the man to die. It was then that it was decided that John Farnell should make a dying declaration. He died the following morning at about five o'clock.

The post mortem revealed that the wound was caused by jagged pieces of lead which had imbedded themselves in the fat around the backbone. Death was caused by inflammation of the liver due to the wound.

Mr. Taylor went on to testify that on the Friday evening after the dying declaration had been made and Allsopp had been taken back to the police station the prisoner had showed him how he made the missiles for the pistol. Calling for a stick he fashioned a piece about the size of a horse bean saying that that was the size of lead he used for the pistol. He also admitted that he loaded it with small stones at times. Mr. Taylor also stated that on the way from the station to Farnell's home Allsopp had told him that "had he had time the night before (one imagines to attack Farnell) the constable would not have been there and he would have been "many a b---- mile away". He also admitted carrying the pistol for some time because the place where he worked was in a lonely spot and he thought it safer to be armed.

The next witness was Abraham Shorter, a lad employed in firing the boilers at the colliery who lived in Red Lane. He stated that he was present when Allsopp arrived at work about twenty minutes past six to relieve Samuel Farnell from the engine, but Samuel had already gone home. The prisoner and Mr. Farnell stood talking for a few minutes in front of the blacksmith's shop and then Mr. Farnell kicked the prisoner with the side of his boot. Several blows were then exchanged before Allsopp was knocked down. The prisoner then got up, walked two or three yards away and then fired at the deceased. The witness ran to fetch Richard Farnell, another of the deceased's sons, and then back to Mr. Farnell who was bleeding from his side but still walking. The prisoner ran off for some twenty yards, but then walked towards the canal.

Under questioning Abraham admitted that he had been too far away to hear the conversation between the prisoner and the deceased being some forty yards off, but clearly saw the fight. Also he had witnessed previous disputes between the men caused by the prisoner being late for work or neglecting his work by letting the engine go too fast. However, he had never known blows being exchanged before.

Abraham also told the hearing that he was not aware that Allsopp carried a pistol with him all the time, but he had seen him fire at doors just for fun. He would load it with small stones, or shot or bits of lead. About three weeks ago he had heard Allsopp threaten to shoot Mr. Farnell or his sons if they came near where he lived. That was after Mr. Farnell had blamed the prisoner for doing something wrong at work.

The next witness was William Stokes, a miner at the colliery, who lived in New Street, Cheslyn Hay. He stated that he was on the pit bank with John Hubery when Allsopp arrived at work. The prisoner came up to them and asked the time. When Hubery told him that the whistle had already blown (meaning it was six o'clock) the prisoner said, "It's too soon. It wants five minutes to six." Leaving him they went to work, but about five minutes later Abraham Shorter asked them if they had seen the fight. The witness looked up and saw Farnell, who was about forty yards away, strike someone and a moment or two later the prisoner got up from behind a small heap of ashes and wiped blood from his nose. They turned back to their work and a minute or two afterwards he heard a pistol fired and heard Allsopp say, "You have got it." Farnell cried out that he had been shot.

The witness then went to fetch Mr. Williams to help him catch Allsopp. As they overtook the prisoner he had a piece of coal in his hand. He put that down and said to them, "Are you come to take me because if you are I'll give you the contents, the same as the other one." However, he did not produce the pistol. At that moment Mr. Farnell shouted that he needed help and the witness went back to help him to the pit office.

When questioned William said that he had never known Allsopp and the deceased quarrel or fight before and had never known Farnell to strike or kick any of the workmen. As to the blood on the prisoner's nose he said that when he overtook him and tried to stop him Allsopp had no blood on his face. In probable defence of the prisoner he admitted that the deceased was a much bigger man and Allsopp might have been frightened during the fight knowing he could not better him.

John Hubery who lived at Mount Pleasant corroborated William's evidence adding that after the shot was fired he saw the deceased struggling towards the engine house and noticed Farnell's shirt which was covered in blood. The witness ran to fetch Mr. Williams and then went to get the police while another man went for the doctor.

John Gregory, junior, stated that about five weeks before the incident the prisoner arrived at work late and Mr. Farnell sent him away on the grounds that he was unfit for work. As he left he turned to the witness and said, "Jack, lad, you mark my word. There will be something the matter before long." When questioned John said Mr. Farnell was not violent towards the workmen and had not struck the prisoner on that occasion.

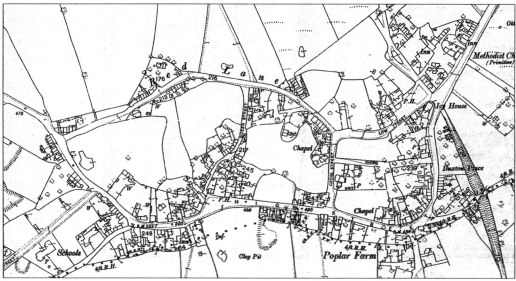

Map 7. Cheslyn Hay 1884.

Fanny Eccleston, who lived in High Street, was present at the death of Mr. Farnell and told the hearing that during the Friday night the deceased had said to her, "Oh dear, for that villain to serve me in this way after I have been a father to him."

The final witness was Constable Samuel Lindop who recounted how he had arrested the prisoner and how he had narrowly missed being shot himself. On their way to the station the prisoner said that he would not have touched Farnell if he had not provoked him – "He struck me and I shot him." At the station he did not reply when charged with attempted murder and when searched the witness found the pistol, still warm, in Allsopp's pocket.

*Constable Lindop lived at the Police House in Town Well Road near Providence House. He had recently married and his wife had not long had their first child (Registered as 1 year old in the 1871 Census.)

All the evidence heard the jury returned a verdict of "Wilful Murder" against James Allsopp and he was committed to trial at Stafford Assizes.

On Tuesday September 20th forty nine year old John Farnell was buried in Cannock Churchyard. There was a very large crowd of mourners and spectators and unusually the choir followed the coffin to the grave where they sang. Later friends of the deceased wrote to the vicar thanking him for the reverent service.

The trial at the Assize Court began on Wednesday December 7th before Baron Cleasby and the fate of James Allsopp would hinge on whether the Prosecution could prove that the prisoner had carried his pistol with intent to shoot and kill his victim. All of the witnesses who gave evidence at the coroner's inquest again repeated their stories with some new ones being heard.

John Hubery repeated his evidence, but under questioning he said that he believed that Allsopp carried a pistol because he was afraid of a man named Hodgson. Apparently that man had been dismissed from the colliery on "account of the prisoner", though he had only heard of that in rumour. Also he admitted that he had not actually seen the start of the fight because of the ash heap, but he thought the prisoner would have no chance against Mr. Farnell in a stand up fight because the deceased was so much bigger.

Having given his evidence Abraham Shorter also added that he knew that the prisoner carried a pistol, but had not heard the story that he did so because he had been shot at. Also he was sure that about half a minute elapsed between the time that the prisoner got up and fired. Besides Abraham another lad, named Eli Pearson, gave the same story as to the fight and shooting.

To show how much of a desperate man Allsopp was the Prosecution asked Constable Lindop to detail all that happened in his arrest of the prisoner. The constable stated that he went in pursuit of the prisoner and caught up with him in Broadlanes. He was walking very fast and when he saw the witness he turned round and fired his pistol at the witness. He managed to dodge the missile, but it still hit his coat. Undeterred he caught hold of the prisoner and there was quite a struggle, but he managed to subdue him and take him into custody.

Questioned as to the struggle the constable said that he had to use his staff on the prisoner and actually hit him with it. That made him bleed "quite freely", but he still had to hit him again to finally quieten him.

After hearing from all the witnesses from the inquest there were two others who had come forward. William Lockett of Queens Street, Cheslyn Hay said that he had accompanied the constable in his search for the prisoner and he witnessed him fire at the constable. He also testified as to the struggle that the constable had to arrest the prisoner. Thomas Williams testified that he had seen the prisoner that day sitting on a rail on the towpath by the canal loading a pistol. He knew that the prisoner was in the habit of carrying a pistol, but had been told by the prisoner himself that it was for killing rats.

Finally Sergeant Barnes of Cannock Police Station stated that he received the prisoner into custody on the night of September 16th and found in his pocket a number of pistol or gun caps, a piece of lead and a piece of iron. The lead had apparently been cut.

In his summing up Mr. Underhill for the Prosecution said that there was no doubt that the prisoner caused the death of the deceased and the only thing to decide was whether the firing of the pistol was committed in passion without thinking of the consequences or if it was done with malice conceived. If it was the intention of the prisoner to injure the deceased then the prisoner ought to be found guilty of murder. However, if the jury were not satisfied that that was the case then they should find the prisoner guilty of manslaughter.

Before his summing up Mr. Smith for the Defence asked James Allsopp to read out his statement of the events. In it he said, "I was going to work. John was standing with his back towards me. I said, "How do you do, John." He replied,

"You -----, you have been blowing the joints off that engine again." I said, "It's a lie," and he kicked me and then struck at me and hit me on the side of the nose and knocked me down on the ground and kicked me three or four times whilst I was on the ground. As soon as I got up he struck at me and knocked me down again. I stood off my distance and said I would make him pay for it."

Having finished Mr. Smith made great play on the fear that must have been in his client's mind and that he had no time to think of what he was going to do to the deceased, but merely acted on impulse. As to the continual carrying of the pistol he said that fear of being attacked by a past workmate made him do it, not the idea of gaining revenge. He contended that the firing of the pistol was caused by passion after considerable provocation. In his mind the jury ought to be considering "justifiable homicide".

In his summing up the judge told the jury that if they were of the opinion that the prisoner was in danger when he committed the act according to the law he was still not justified in using a pistol to defend himself. If they were convinced that was the case then their finding should be one of manslaughter. However, if they considered the prisoner had acted with intent to kill then the verdict should be murder.

After a few minutes deliberation the jury returned a verdict of "Manslaughter". The judge said that he "perfectly agreed", but it was nevertheless his duty to pass a severe sentence on the prisoner and James Allsopp was given ten years penal servitude.

Before the court was dismissed Mr. Underhill asked the judge if he would grant Constable Lindop a reward of £20 for his bravery. The judge gladly complied.

★The next episode happened at the same colliery. However, it may not have been at the same pit or shaft. Cannock and Wyrley Colliery Company was a series of mines or shafts in the Cheslyn Hay and Wyrley area, the Grove being the deepest. The mine where Farnell worked was not stated at the inquest or the trial. No. 6 Pit in the following episode was nicknamed the Palmerston Colliery, possibly after the Prime Minister of the day when it was first sunk.

On Friday June 6th, 1879 Arthur Cartwright arrived at Mr. George Wootton's grocer's shop in High Street in Cheslyn Hay for some tobacco and having purchased it he proceeded to his work place at the Wyrley-Cannock Colliery. Once there he went into the engine house and started a conversation with Cornelius Buckley, an engine-tenter man at the pit. All seemed perfectly friendly, but as Cornelius bent to examine the engine a loud report from a gun was heard and Cornelius felt a sharp pain in the back of his scalp. Not realising at first what exactly had happened he rose to talk to Cartwright, but the man had disappeared. It was only then that he knew that his workmate had in fact shot at him.

As for Arthur Cartwright, he raced away, throwing the gun on to a dunghill by the pit stables as he went, and headed for his lodgings. Once there he calmly washed, smartened himself up and then left to seek the nearest policeman at Wyrley Police Station and deliver himself into the hands of the law. However, before he had managed to reach the police station another man named Edward Stallard had gone there to tell them of the shooting. Unfortunately for both men Constable Davis was not at home (police stations were frequently part of an officer's home) and so Stallard offered to walk to Cannock Police Station with Arthur.

Arthur agreed and the two set off. As they walked along Stallard began to get worried in case Cartwright still had the pistol on his person and so when they met a young man named Eccleston he suggested that the young man might like to walk with them. The three continued their walk and subsequently met up with a police sergeant. Stallard then suggested that Arthur might like to give himself up to the sergeant, but Arthur simply said, "We have come so far let us go all the way to the station." He also suggested that Stallard might like to treat him to "a little beer as it might be some time before he might get another taste". Finally they reached the police station and Cartwright gave himself up.

On Monday June 9th Cartwright appeared before the magistrates at Cannock, but because Buckley had not sufficiently recovered to appear (apparently as many as twenty shots were lodged in his head) the case was not discussed and the prisoner was remanded until the following Monday.

Before the magistrates session happened news of the attack obviously spread around the district and rumours began to circulate as to why Cartwright should shoot Buckley. A man from the Potteries, he had never quite fitted in with village life in Cheslyn Hay despite living there for about five years and had seemingly blamed Buckley's brother for causing him to be discharged from his work at the pit. Rumour had it that because he could not find Cornelius's brother Cartwright had simply taken his revenge on the first member of the family that he saw. Would the hearing find out the truth?

The case was finally heard on Monday June 23rd, 1879 before Lord Hatherton and Colonel Harrison and Arthur Wagg (his real name) was charged with attempting to murder Cornelius Buckley. (It was not uncommon for people to change names, especially if they moved into another area. It was not necessarily used to hide a notorious past, though it could help.)

Mr. Glover appeared for the Prosecution and his first witness was Cornelius Buckley himself who lived in the Wyrley Cannock Colliery houses in Dunduck Lane (now Dundalk Lane). Though very much recovered from his horrific experience he presented a sorry sight with his head still heavily bandaged. He testified that he was an engine-tenter at Wyrley-Cannock Colliery No. 6 Pit and on the afternoon of Friday June 6th he went on duty at 5 p.m. About a quarter of an hour later the prisoner arrived at the engine room and began talking to him in a "friendly manner" until about 7 o'clock. About that time, when the witness's back was turned, there was a sudden loud report from a pistol and the witness immediately felt a blow to the back of his head.

He fell forward and when he got up he put his hand to the back of his head and seeing blood exclaimed, "Oh dear, there has somebody shot me, Arthur." (I bet those were not his actual words, but Cornelius had cleaned them up for the court.) The prisoner replied, "Has there?" and then brushed passed the witness and ran off along the canal side. Realising what had happened and who might have done the deed the witness raised the alarm.

Although it might be obvious to Cornelius and everyone hearing the story that Arthur Wagg was the guilty party the court still had to make absolutely certain - people have been known to admit to crimes they have not committed - and so other witnesses were essential The first of those was William Hemmingsley, a shepherd living at Saredon. He stated that he was near the colliery on the day and heard the gun being fired and rushed to where he thought the shot had come from. As he got nearer he saw the prisoner run down the canal side from the direction of No. 6 Pit. Continuing on towards the pit he met Cornelius who said, "Will, I am shot." He was bleeding from a wound in the back of his head, but despite that he pointed at the prisoner and accused him of the shooting. The witness then told the hearing that he ran after the prisoner, but could not catch him and so went to the colliery office and fetched Edward Stallard.

Edward Stallard, clerk at the colliery, who also lived at the colliery houses, said that from the information received he went to the police station at Wyrley, but the officer was out. While he was there the prisoner arrived and asked, "What do you want?" Wagg then pulled his watchguard off his neck and gave it, along with the watch, to the police officer's wife. The witness then proceeded to walk with the prisoner to Cannock Police Station.

As they were walking along the witness noticed blood on the prisoner's hand and asked how it got there. The prisoner replied, "I do not know," to which the witness replied, "What did you shoot him with, a gun or a pistol?" Wagg answered, "With a pistol which you will find on the manure heap near Eccleston's Stable." The witness then told the hearing that he asked Wagg why he did it and the prisoner's reply was, "The man who does me an injury I shall try to do him one", adding that Buckley had got him discharged from his work.

Sergeant Cockerell of Cannock Police stated that he took Wagg into custody and questioned him about the shooting. After charging him with the shooting of Buckley and cautioning him the prisoner simply replied, "I have nothing to say, only that he was the fault of me being out of a situation." He was then searched and in his coat pocket were found gun caps and shot.

Constable Preston testified that he and the sergeant discovered the pistol used in the shooting on the manure heap near to the engine house at the pit and it appeared to have been recently discharged. The cock was down on the nipple, on which was an exploded cap. The stock was shaken, apparently from the force of overloading. The constable went on to state that on Tuesday, June 10th while taking the prisoner from Cannock to Stafford he was reading the local paper when the prisoner asked, "Is my case in?" The witness replied that it was and then read out the report to the prisoner. On hearing it Wagg said, "That is not right what is in the paper. They said there were 26 shots in his head, but I know better. There were only 20 for I counted them one by one as I put them in the pistol." (Pistols had to be loaded with individual shots and not cartridges.)

The final witness was Doctor Mockett who stated that he visited Cornelius at about 8 p.m. on June 6th and found a shot wound in the back of his head, covering a space of about two and a half inches. There was also a lacerated wound with about 20 shot marks and the skull was injured. There were powder marks on the left ear which indicated the closeness of the assailant.

Having heard all the witnesses the magistrates asked Wagg if he had anything to add. He simply said, "I have nothing to say. I do not know why I did it. I was much put about through leaving my place." (Apparently the Colliery Company were laying off men as they often did in the summer months due to a slow down in trade and because Wagg had only been there a short time he was one chosen to go. Strangely Wagg blamed Buckley rather than the pit owners.) That said the magistrates committed him to the Assizes.

That court met on Friday, July 18th before Mr. Justice Hawkins. With the evidence completed the judge asked Wagg if he had anything to say in his defence. He simply said that the shooting was accidental. Had he intended to shoot Cornelius Buckley "he should have loaded the pistol with a bullet. He had fired at a bird and accidentally shot the prosecutor."

However, he was found guilty and the judge declared that there were "no mitigating circumstances whatsoever" and sentenced Wagg to seven years penal servitude.

If that case could be one of attempted murder the following just proves how unwise it is to allow the general public to carry weapons. What began as a marital row could so easily have turned into a case of murder. On the night of Monday August 31st, 1885 two men were walking home from the local Wakes when they overheard a husband and wife arguing. When the wife ran from the house the two decided to intervene on her behalf and attack the husband. In his defence he then fired at them to scare them away, unfortunately hitting one of the men.

At the September Sessions of the Petty Court at Cannock, before Mr. Gilpin and Mr. Briscoe, Alfred Lloyd was charged with shooting young George Ridgway with intent to do him bodily harm.

Twenty one year old George Ridgway of 4 Company Buildings was first to give evidence. He said that on that Monday at about 10.30 p.m. he and his friend, David James, were on their way home in Cheslyn Hay and as they neared Lloyd's house they heard cries of "Murder" which seemed to come from the house. A little further along the road they met Moses Lockett and then Mrs. Lloyd appeared from the house. She came up to them and complained that her husband had assaulted her; she had blood on her head to prove it. At that moment Alfred Lloyd came out of the house and accused them of making his wife worse by listening to her. He then produced a gun and fired at the men, hitting George in the thumb.

However, Lloyd had got himself a solicitor, Mr. Loxton, who began to question George over the affair. George was adamant that he had not gone into the Lloyd house, nor had he even gone to the door. He was also adamant that there had been no struggle between anybody while he was there and certainly "no scuffle". He was insistent that when he was shot he was standing in the road and Moses Lockett was with him. It was dark and so he could not see exactly who was present, but was sure that David James did not go past the house nor did he go inside.

Mr. Loxton persisted and once more George denied being in the house, insisting that he stayed on the road. He added, "I was just in front of the prisoner's house when I saw him come out through the door. He was coming out of a lighted up room into the dark and only said that we would make his wife worse and then he fired." He also denied that there had been any bad feeling between him and Lloyd in the past and swore that the prisoner did not even know he was one of the men when he fired.

As to the actual shooting George stated that there was only one shot and that struck him. Lloyd was standing between his house and the wooden railings which separated the garden from the road when he fired. After the shot the prisoner's son went by him.

Seemingly irrelevant to the case Mr. Loxton asked George if he were in any other trouble in the village to which George had to admit that he was to appear before the magistrates that same day for committing an assault on one Charles Jones.

The next witness was David James, a miner from Cheslyn Hay. He said that he was with George Ridgway on the night in question and they had come from The Star at Wedges Mills where there had been a Wake. He heard Mrs. Lloyd scream "Murder" and when she appeared she had blood on her face. Then the prisoner came from the house and fired at them saying he would "blow our ---- brains out". At that point the witness knocked the gun out of the prisoner's hand. Again questioned by Mr. Loxton James was also adamant that was no scuffle while he was present and that they did not go into the house.

Eighteen year old Moses Lockett from Queens Street testified that he met up with Ridgway and James near to the Lloyd's house. There they met Mrs. Lloyd who was shouting out "Murder" and she told them that her husband had struck her with a saucepan and knife. After that evidence he merely told exactly the same story as James and Ridgway.

Sergeant Upton stated that from information given he and Constables Hodgetts and Daley went to the prisoner's home later that same night. However, before they arrived there they met the prisoner who told them that he had had a row with his wife. He also told them about the gun and that a man named Holt had taken it away. Once retrieved from Holt's house Lloyd was arrested. The sergeant also took away two pieces of wood from the railings outside the

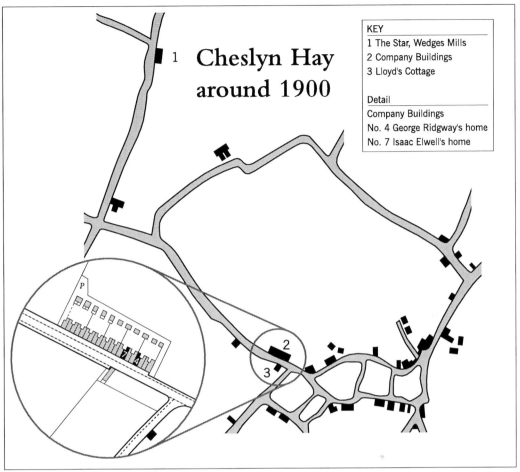

Map 8.

Lloyd home which had been shattered by the shot. Finally he testified that when he saw Lloyd he still had marks of blood on his face.

It was then the turn of sixteen year old Levi Lloyd to give his version of the episode. He stated that he had seen the witnesses assaulting and kicking his father.

In a slightly unusual turn of events the prisoner then became the prosecutor and the witnesses the defendants. George Ridgway, David James and Isaac Elwell were then charged with assaulting Alfred Lloyd. (Elwell had been present at the fracas, but had decided not to give evidence against Lloyd. The Elwells lived at 7 Company Buildings. Strangely Isaac does not appear on the 1881 Census though there were three Elwell lads mentioned. Sometimes newspapers got a name wrong or Isaac may have been his second name.)

24. Company Buildings at the start of demolition in the early 1970s.

Alfred Lloyd then took the stand and stated that he lived at Cheslyn Hay opposite the Company Buildings and on the night of August 31st he and his wife had quarrelled. As a result of the row his wife left the house and about ten minutes later James and Ridgway came in. Elwell only put his head inside the door, but did not enter. James then grabbed hold of the witness by the collar and said, "Come out, we will ...... kill you." At that point he and Ridgway dragged the witness outside and as they did Elwell struck him.

Once outside the prisoners knocked the witness down and kicked him, but he managed to escape back into the house. James then shouted, "Let's get him out again and we will give him some more!" The witness then told the hearing that he picked up his gun to protect himself and told his attackers that he would fire if they did not leave him alone. He then fired into the garden, as he thought, but the shot went higher than he intended. It was dark and he could not see clearly. James then knocked the gun from his hand and knocked him down again and they started to kick him once more.

Fearful for his life the witness then shouted "Murder" and the men ran off. However, James returned and asked, "What is the matter?" to which the witness replied, "You know all about it. You are one of those who have been knocking me about and I have sent for the police."

Strangely the next witness to defend Alfred's actions was Rebecca, his wife. She testified that there had indeed been a row with her husband and at about 10.20 p.m. she had left the house. She had passed Ridgway and James in the road and they had gone through her gate and rushed into her house. (Rebecca made no mention of telling the men about her quarrel.) She immediately went back home and found Ridgway and James with their hands around her husband's collar and they were punching him.

Elwell struck him on the back of his head.

The assailants then dragged her husband into the road and got him to the ground. He got free and returned to the house and got his gun. He then threatened the men and, being very frightened, the witness went for the police with her son. They went different ways to his home, but he was not in. When she returned to the house she saw a great deal of blood on the window and on her husband's shirt. He wiped the blood on to a cloth and some of it must have got on to her apron. All those articles were produced in court.

When Sergeant Upton arrived at the scene he found a carving knife and asked if it was the one used in the scuffle. The witness told him that she was not sure. When he questioned her further the witness had to admit that she did not know if the knife had been used in the attack at all or if it caused the loss of blood.

The magistrates had heard enough. They declared that they did not believe Mrs. Lloyd's statement at all and were positive that a serious quarrel had taken place between her and her husband and upon her screaming "Murder" the defendants had tried to help her. However, they had "exceeded their duty". Also they did not believe that Alfred Lloyd had fired the gun "for any other purpose than to frighten the defendants". Consequently they dismissed the charge against Lloyd and inflicted a fine of 10 shillings each on the defendants, whom they warned never again to interfere with a man and his wife.

That brought to an end Cheslyn Hay's fifteen year brush with the Wild West.

SIMPLY WORKED TO DEATH
Colton/Hednesford 1895

Working class families had no option but to send their children out to work to make ends meet as the father's wage was barely sufficient to keep a family in food, clothing and payment of bills. Most boys in our area, some as young as twelve, went down the pit or into factories whilst the girls frequently found themselves in service. Life in service was hard with long hours and the daily drudgery of menial tasks, but at least board and lodging was found and meals probably more regular than could be expected at home. So what went drastically wrong in the case of fourteen year old Annie Bridgart from Green Heath, Hednesford?

On the morning of Thursday, June 6th, 1895 a farmer's cart pulled up outside the home of the Bridgarts at Green Heath. Lying in the back on some straw was Annie in a dreadful condition. She was very dirty and had far too much clothing on considering the time of year and it was buttoned up tightly. It was also obvious that she was extremely ill and so, with the help of the young lad who drove the cart, George Bridgart, Annie's brother, helped the hapless girl into the house where they laid her on the sofa. Immediately the doctor was summoned, but Annie died before the day was out.

Rumours soon spread around the neighbourhood of Green Heath and Mount Street that the girl had died from severe treatment by her master and mistress who kept Newlands Farm at Colton near Rugeley. Gossip had it that she had been frequently beaten, even horse whipped and kicked. However, there were others who talked of Annie's habit of telling lies and would not believe the stories preferring to treat them with the proverbial "grain of salt". Only a coroner's inquest would suffice to stop the tongues from wagging.

That inquest began on Monday, June 10th at the West Cannock Inn before Mr. Morgan with Mr. W. Coltman as foreman of the jury. The first to give evidence was Mary Bridgart, wife of Thomas Bridgart and sister-in-law to Annie, who lived in Green Heath and had been the one who identified the body. She stated that Annie had been employed by Mr. Myatt of Newlands Farm for about five months and had not been back home all that time. On the morning of the tragedy Annie had arrived back in a trap at about 10.15 a.m. and was in a dirty condition. She had a great deal of clothing on which was fastened very tightly.

25. West Cannock Inn, Mount Street, Hednesford.
Now the Bell and Bottle, it first opened in 1871.

When talking to Annie the deceased had told her that her master had horse whipped her the week before and had kicked her which had caused a bruise on the back of her right thigh. He had also threatened to kick her on the morning of her return home if she did not "hold up to have her clothing on". Miss Myatt, sister to the farm owner, had struck her on the same morning. She also told the witness that her master would not let her write home unless he or his sister saw the letters first.

Mary told the hearing that Doctor Edmondson had been called immediately and had treated the girl, but she died the same night at about 11.00 p.m.

When questioned by the jury Mary said that the deceased had told her that she had not been to bed the night before her return after working all day. On the following morning her master and mistress had got her up very early and wanted her to work, but realising how ill she was they wanted to have her taken home. They forced her to have her clothes on leaving her night dress on and tying up the sleeves. The deceased also told her that she had been ill since the Monday and could not work despite her master's complaints.

* The parents of young Annie had both died and it was Annie's brothers and sisters who thought it best that she be put in service as there would be no one at home to care for her while they were at work.

lying in the back on some straw, but there was a cushion under her head. The farm lad who brought her simply said, "I have brought your sister home," and when asked where she was he replied, "She is in the bottom of the cart nearly dead". He then took her into the house and laid her on the sofa and went out again to question the lad. The boy told him that the deceased had been ill since the Monday and "they" had given her soap suds to drink and mustard and water to make her sick. After that George went to fetch the doctor.

He told the court that he had not heard his sister make any statement about her treatment or the Myatts. He did, however, say that he had never received any letters from her, but another sister had though they could not be read because they were covered with ink.

Emma Brookes, a neighbour, stated that she was fetched to the Bridgarts' house to see the girl at about 1.45 p.m. on the Thursday and found

1891 Cannock Census Returns				
Street/Area	Name	Age	Occupation	Where born
Green Heath	Samuel Bridgart	48	Widower	Penkridge
	Thomas Bridgart	24	Railway Plate Layer	Birmingham
	Mary Anne do.	20	Domestic Servant	Birmingham
	George do.	18	Bricklayers Labourer	Cannock
	William do.	16	Coal Miner	Cannock
	Samuel do.	14	Brickyard Labourer	Penkridge
	Emma do.	12	Scholar	Penkridge
	Annie do.	10	do.	Penkridge
	Lucy do.	7	do.	Penkridge
	Ellen do.	5		Cannock
	Ann do.	3		Cannock

* Samuel, the father, was already ill by the time of this Census and died a few years later. By 1895 Thomas had married and it was his wife who testified at the hearing.

Few streets in the Green Heath area, with the exception of Abbey Street, had adopted names by 1891 and so it is difficult to say exactly where the family lived.

George Bridgart, Annie's brother and also living at Green Heath, told the hearing that he was at home when the trap arrived. His sister was

her in bed. The doctor was still there and the witness put a poultice on the girl's left side over the bruise. The girl's clothing was in a most filthy condition as was the girl herself. Her underclothes looked as though they had been worn for a month or two.

When questioned Emma said that the deceased had said that she had been "worked to death" though she had not made any complaint to her master or mistress. Emma also said that she had "laid out" the corpse and had seen a bruise

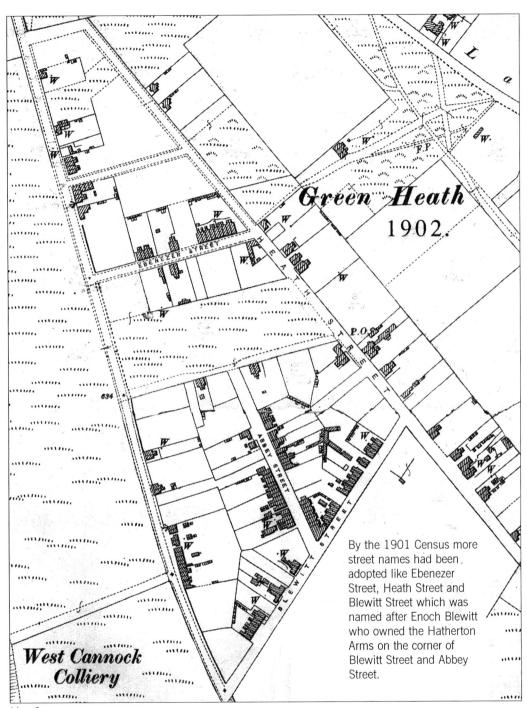

Green Heath
1902.

West Cannock
Colliery

By the 1901 Census more street names had been adopted like Ebenezer Street, Heath Street and Blewitt Street which was named after Enoch Blewitt who owned the Hatherton Arms on the corner of Blewitt Street and Abbey Street.

Map 9.

on the right side which was as large as the witness's hand.

Emily (Emma) Bridgart, Annie's sister, stated that she was also at home when the cart arrived and her sister was in a filthy condition. Her sister had told her that Mr. Myatt had ill-treated her and Miss Myatt had hit her that morning because she would not stand up to be dressed. Emily also told of the letters that she had received and of a visit she had made to the farm.

In a letter about two months ago her sister had complained that Mr. Myatt had tried to indecently assault her and because she had refused and told Miss Myatt he had hit her. The witness said she had no idea how her sister had managed to get that letter to her because every letter she had written had to be inspected by either her master or mistress. However, every letter that she did receive was covered with ink blots. As to the visit Emily told the hearing that she had gone to see Annie about a month ago, but could not see her alone, either Miss Myatt or the other servant had to be there. When she asked to see her alone she was told that she was too busy and had work to do. Feeling awkward the witness left to catch her train.

When questioned about the letters and the accusation of indecency Emily said that her sister had said not to ask the Myatts about it as it had not happened again. Her brother had also read the letters and advised her to burn them. As to the visit Emily said that she had been at the farm from 3.30 p.m. until 7.45 p.m. and her sister was very busy all the time and was never alone. She did not have anything to eat while the witness was there. It was after that visit that the letters stopped altogether.

At that point the inquest had to be stopped because Mr. Morgan had another inquiry at the Cross Keys at midday, but it reopened in the afternoon. Dr. Edmondson was first to give his evidence. He testified that he had been sent for to see the deceased at about 11.00 a.m., but he was out at the time and so arrived at the Bridgarts' home at around 1.30 p.m. He found the girl in bed, extremely ill and suffering from a high fever which made her breathing very rapid. He diagnosed pneumonia of the left lung and, although he treated her as best he could, he informed her sister that there was very little hope of recovery. However, as far as he was concerned the deceased did not know that she was about to die.

He told the hearing that he only saw her the once before she died and was not told of the bruises, but the deceased had said that she had been mistreated. When he made the post mortem he discovered a small bruise on her right hip which was about a week old. He thought it might have been caused by a blow, a kick or a fall, but was "not of a serious matter and unconnected with the cause of death".

Internally he found inflammation of the left lung and slight congestion on the right one. There was a little redness in the stomach such as what might have been caused by an irritant like mustard, but not caused by an irritant like poison. The actual cause of death was heart failure brought on by the pneumonia. The pneumonia he estimated had been probably been going on for two or three days before death.

When questioned the doctor said that "to an ordinary person it would be distinguishable from an ordinary cold" as there must have been "intense difficulty of breathing and feverishness" and he had never seen a more acute case on a first visit. He thought it "highly improper to have sent a person so suffering in an open carriage for a distance of about nine miles". In his estimation the journey had made matters worse and had "accelerated death". He was certain that had she remained at the farm and received medical treatment there she would still be alive as she was a strong girl and would have been able to throw off the attack.

Questioned further he stated that he "could not positively say she would have recovered, but in all human probability she would have done so, especially had she lain up on the day when she was first taken ill". Furthermore he did not know how she could have done her work in such a state.

The next witness was George Williscroft, a farm lad employed by Mr. Myatt. He said that on the orders of his master he drove the deceased to Green Heath on the Thursday morning. Mr. Myatt had told the witness to drive her home in the trap as she was very bad and it would be better for her if she were at home. She was laid on some straw with a cushion under her head and a rug over her. Mr. and Mrs. Myatt put her in the trap. They told him to tell her brother that the girl had been trying to poison herself with butter of antimony that they used for dressing the horses' feet. The journey took from 8.30 in the morning until 10.20.

He testified that the deceased had never complained to him of being ill-treated and he had never seen her treated badly. Neither had she complained of his master trying to indecently assault her. Also as a rule the girl had her meals at the same time as the witness and he was sure that she had nothing to complain of in that respect as the food was ample; neither was she overworked. Another servant told him that the deceased had told her that she had been taking poison.

As to the administering of soap suds and mustard by Miss Myatt, he admitted that he had seen it done because of the poison the deceased had said that she had taken. However, he had never heard the deceased threaten to take poison, but he had heard her say she wished she were dead so that she would have no more work to do. So far as he was concerned "she was a very idle girl".

To endeavour to clear up the notion of poison Dr. Edmondson was recalled and questioned by Mr. Goscomb, a jury member. The doctor said that if the deceased had taken much of the antimony he should have been able to detect it, but there was no sign of it. However, if she had had the mustard and water immediately afterwards the vomiting may have cleared it from her stomach.

Alice Handford, domestic servant to the Myatts and the one referred to by George Williscroft, was next in the stand. She testified that on Tuesday June 4th the deceased rose at about 4.15 a.m. and some time later the witness found her heaving. When asked what was wrong the deceased said that she had taken some poison. Alice told Miss Myatt who gave the deceased soap suds and wanted to call a doctor, but the deceased would have none of it. By the Thursday morning the deceased was worse and was sent home.

When questioned about the deceased Alice told the hearing that she was "an idle and troublesome girl and very dirty" and on several occasions had been found drunk. It was Miss Myatt's fault that she was kept at the farm because Mr. Myatt had wanted to send her home some time ago, but her mistress had pleaded that she be allowed to stay. Also Alice said that the girl had not wanted to go home as she was ill-treated there. As to being overworked Alice said that after the Tuesday episode the deceased had not worked again until she was sent home.

It was then the turn of the Myatts to give their side of the story. Eli Myatt, owner of Newlands Farm, stated that the deceased had been in his employ for about five months and he had sent her home on Thursday June 6th because he had been informed that she had taken some poison. He had wanted her to leave on the Tuesday, but his sister had told him that the girl had said that she felt better after being given something to make her vomit and that she might recover. He knew of no reason why the girl should want to take poison, only that she did not like work. In fact, he thought her "a very idle little girl".

On the Wednesday morning the girl was much the same, but by the Thursday he thought it best for her to go home. He did not notice any cold, only that she sounded a little hoarse, but he put that down to all the vomiting. He thought it better that she see a doctor when she arrived home. As to the idea of him indecently assaulting the girl, he testified that it was "a great untruth" and he had found her to be "untruthful, idle and very dirty over her work". In fact he would have sent her home long before only his sister had persuaded him that the girl might improve.

When questioned over the accusations of violence towards the deceased he swore that he had never ill-used her and had never heard of the accusations of kicking or indecent assault before. As to the letters he stated that she could write home whenever she liked. As for the idea that she was overworked he said that she got up between four and five in the morning and went to bed at eight o'clock. She only really had about four hours work during the day. Also there were three meals a day provided and the girl had free access to all meat.

★ If those meals were to believed, and there was no evidence to prove otherwise, then Annie was being given far more than most of the working classes might have eaten during an average day, even if they worked in factories or mines.

To add further doubt to the character of Annie Mr. Myatt said that she often got drunk. It was her job to draw ale for the farm workers, but she often drank some herself. That problem had not come to his notice until about three weeks previously when he saw her drunk, but his sister had persuaded him to let her stay and for her to sort out the problem.

The final witness was Miss Hannah Myatt

who insisted on giving evidence. (Remember accused people did not have to give evidence at the coroner's hearing.) She stated that on Tuesday June 4th Alice Handford had sent for her and then told her that the deceased had been taking poison. She immediately saw the girl who admitted it and then asked the witness if she could give her something for it. Soap suds and water were prepared and administered which made the girl vomit an oily substance. She then gave her more soap suds and a weak mixture of mustard and water which made the girl vomit several times.

The witness did not call the doctor because the girl said that she was a little better and she was afraid that the doctor might use a stomach pump or punish her for taking the poison. When she was a little better the deceased went down the cellar, but on returning she was sick again; she had been drinking a lot of ale. On the Wednesday the girl was somewhat better and did what work she could, but by the Thursday as she had not improved her brother said that it would be better if she were sent home.

When questioned Miss Myatt said that she had noticed that the deceased had got a "thorough cold and complained of soreness in the chest", but thought it was not serious. As to her behaviour towards the girl she swore that she had never struck her or threatened her with a horse whip and had never looked at the girl's letters from home. Also the girl had as much to eat as she liked, but was forbidden ale. However, it had come to the witness's notice that the girl had "got to the barrel". The girl had never made any complaint to her about indecent assault.

Questioned about the way the girl was sent home Miss Myatt stated that she thought she had dealt kindly in sending her there. As to the manner in which she appeared Miss Myatt said that the girl's clothing was filthy because she did not wash them. However, the body linen was clean. In fact the girl was so dirty she had had to wash her in a tub and clean her hair on occasion.

At that point the coroner asked why they had kept the girl for so long if she was so bad to which Miss Myatt replied that she did not know the girl "had such naughty (untruthful) ways". Turning to Doctor Edmondson he asked if he wished to modify his opinion as to the cause of

death after he had heard all the evidence. The doctor said that he did not.

All evidence heard the coroner summed up the case which he described as "most curious", not clarified as there was "a lot of evidence of an unreliable character". He thought the evidence of Alice Handford "very straightforward which threw more light on the case than any other". As to the statements made against the Myatts by the deceased they were uncorroborated and "would not be admissible in a criminal court because they were not made with knowledge of immediate death". (Had the Bridgarts got Annie to make a dying declaration in front of a witness matters could have been worse for the Myatts.)

Continuing he said that "there was certainly great laxity of duty on the part of the master and mistress and in his opinion they were guilty of a great error in judgement", but whether there was anything more than unthoughtfulness was up to the jury to decide. Perhaps the possibility of the taking of poison had clouded their judgement and the girl's fear of seeing a doctor. However, "under all circumstances they were very negligent in their duties".

The jury, without any private deliberation, came to the decision that the deceased had died from pneumonia accelerated by the rough treatment in not sending for a doctor and instead treating her at her home and the rough manner in which she was sent home. They asked the coroner to "severely censure" Mr. and Miss Myatt.

The coroner did exactly that, but Miss Myatt began to argue that the girl was not dying when she left the farm. He stopped her immediately pointing out that the medical evidence proved that she was and they ought to have known it. He refused to let the Myatts have anything more to say and dismissed them. As they left the court the crowd of women gathered there made their feelings towards the Myatts clearly known. They were positive the pair were lucky to escape a trial.

But that was not the end of the affair. On Monday July 15th they appeared before the magistrates at the Rugeley Petty Sessions charged with "wilfully ill-treating and neglecting Annie Bridgart". The Bench was chaired by Sir Charles Forster with Messrs. Bonney, Anderson, Smith and Hislop while Mr. Burrows of Walsall prosecuted for the Walsall and District Branch of the National

26. Constable Leslie Owens. Born in Brereton around 1898 he joined the local police force around 1920 and finally ended up at Moss Side, Manchester where he retired in the 1950s.

Society for the Prevention of Cruelty to Children and Mr. Payne defended the Myatts.

The case began with Mr. Payne arguing that the court should only hear one of the supposed offences and not try to defend his clients' actions over the whole period that the deceased was employed. To defend themselves for any actions over such a period was, he thought, impossible. Mr. Lewis for the Prosecution argued that where the offences were continuous they should all be tried. Payne then asked the magistrates if they were prepared to sit through a lengthy trial which could take into account any actions between January and June of that year. Finally he submitted when the Prosecution made it clear that they would only deal in depth with the main issue, that of the events of the week of June 6th.

Having gone through all the evidence given at the inquest Mr. Lewis argued that "sending the girl home in the state she was, without taking medical advice, was ill-treatment and likely to cause the girl serious injury". Also he contended the way she was sent off "was an offence against the Act". Continuing he stated that as the girl had no parents "the defendants took in a sense

the place of parents to the girl" and should have seen that she was properly fed, washed and with clean clothes as well as looking after her physical welfare.

Mr. Payne for the Defence cross-examined Dr. Edmondson concerning his diagnosis, but the doctor remained adamant that had the girl been treated at the farm she might very well be still alive.

The only new witness at the court was Sergeant Burgess who told the court that he had gone to Newlands Farm on June 8th and interviewed Miss Myatt about the horse whipping incident. Miss Myatt said that the deceased "was a naughty girl for saying that" and that she had never ill-treated her. What she had admitted was throwing some water on the girl one morning when she found her asleep on the scullery floor. She also admitted administering the soap suds to make the girl ill after hearing of the poison.

All the evidence heard the magistrates agreed that so far as the charge of ill-treatment was concerned there was "nothing to complain of" and all the servants "seemed to have been treated above the ordinary". At the same time they agreed that "there had been grave indiscretion shown by the defendants in sending the girl home, though they did not appear to have known what the cause of the illness was". Therefore, "in their opinion it did not constitute an offence" and the case was dismissed.

27. The first picture shows the young Constable Frederick Barker, born in 1899 and stationed at Burton-upon-Trent after WW1. He married in 1922 and moved to Rugeley.
28. The second picture shows Barker, by now a Sergeant, in the mid-thirties. It is thought the picture was taken possibly in Cannock.

One wonders just how far the case might have gone had not the girl been from the working classes and the defendants from the middle class. Also it goes to show that, despite the new law concerning children, they were still considered lesser citizens than adults and of lesser importance.

Footnote:- The Myatt family were originally yeoman farmers in North Staffordshire. In the 1870's Simon and Hannah Myatt had moved to Newland Grange with their son, Eli, and daughter, Hannah. Brother and sister remained at the farm and in the 1891 Census are recorded as having 2 domestic servants and 3 farm labourers. Hannah died in 1904 and Eli in 1919, both buried at Colton. Newland Grange was a sizeable farm in the hamlet of Newlands, part of the Parish of Colton. (Information from members of the Colton History Society.)

THE TRAGEDY OF THE GREEN DRAGON
Hatherton 1891

All parents have a dread of leaving their offspring at home for the first time as the family holiday no longer has that attraction for ageing children. Will the home still be there when they get back, just how many friends will be invited to that inevitable party and are they still too young to look after themselves? Will those lads, who seem to argue with one another all the time, control their tempers without the presence of either parent or will they simply "kill" one another? A holiday may seem like a lifetime, but what parent would think twice about just leaving them alone for a day or a few hours.

George Whitehouse and his wife, Matilda, certainly did not as they set off to visit friends in Chadsmoor, only three miles away on the Thursday morning of August 20th, 1891. They had been away from the public house, the Green Dragon, before and left the two lads to look after the place, providing they did not serve any customers or play with the gun that was always left hanging on hooks in the back kitchen. So they were astonished when they arrived back between three and four in the afternoon to find quite a crowd of people standing around their home and even more shocked when they discovered that their son, Guy, was missing.

William Whitehouse, the eighteen year old son of George by his first marriage, was immediately questioned as to eleven year old Guy's whereabouts. William blurted out that he had been outside the public house feeding the turkeys when he had heard the report of a gun coming from the passage in the building. On entering the house he saw smoke, but could not see anyone. Being too frightened to enter he had called a neighbour, Mr. Adderley, who searched the building. He could not find Guy either. Then William told his father that he had seen a

travelling show pass the public house early in the afternoon and thought that Guy might have gone off with the showmen.

While the rest of the people searched the surroundings at Hatherton George Whitehouse went off to Brewood, the direction in which the show had gone, with another neighbour, Mr. Hawley, and William. Arriving there they contacted the local police and then began to question the travelling showmen. Having no success George returned home accompanied by Constable Hall of Shareshill and they once more searched the building, but found nothing. Again William was questioned and again he told the same story. Then, as it was dark, they called off their search until the next morning.

The following morning George, William and Mr. Adderley travelled to Brewood again to ask further questions and search the show again, but still found nothing. They returned to the public house, accompanied by Sergeant Whitehurst and he and Constable Hall began a systematic search of the whole building. It was not long before Hall discovered the body of young Guy on top of the oven in the building used for brewing. It had not been discovered earlier as the room was badly lit and the body almost hidden behind some sticks.

William was immediately sent to Cannock to fetch a doctor and Sergeant Upton from Cannock Police Station. Strangely, as would be found out later, when William was stopped by several people and asked about his brother's whereabouts, he replied that the lad had not been found. (Nerves perhaps?) Dr. Taylor, the locum for Dr. Butter, and Sergeant Upton accompanied the boy back to the Green Dragon and examined the corpse. It was quickly removed for a post mortem.

That completed Sergeant Upton turned his attention to William and once more the lad was questioned as to his brother's movements. Suspicious of the young man, the sergeant made him write down his statement, and unsatisfied with the results he arrested William and took him back to Cannock Police Station and locked him up. At first the young man stuck to his original statement, but after time he began to change his account of what had happened on that fatal dinner time. On Monday, August 24th William was taken before the local magistrates and formally remanded until three o'clock on the Wednesday until the inquest into the death of Guy Craig had taken place.

*Mrs. Whitehouse had been married previously to a Mr. Arrowsmith and when she married George Whitehouse young Guy retained his mother's maiden name, despite being welcomed into the Whitehouse family.

The inquest began on Tuesday August 25th at the Green Dragon before W. Morgan, Esq. Major Orwell, the magistrate who had remanded William, was present as were a large crowd of reporters (the crime had been widely reported throughout the country).

The first witness was a distraught George Whitehouse who began by saying that he had identified the corpse as that of his eleven year old stepson, Guy James Craig. He continued by telling the hearing that on Thursday, August 20th he had gone with his wife to Chadsmoor to visit friends and had left William and Guy to look after the house. They were not to serve spirits to anyone and not to touch the gun which hung up in the back kitchen. He swore that to the best of his knowledge neither gun barrel was loaded, but "would not swear positively".

When he returned home he saw a number of people around his home and soon learned that his son, Guy, was lost. He went into the house and got the gun to examine it and found it in its usual place. Neither barrel seemed to have been discharged, but he had asked his son if he had been messing with it. His son had said, "No, father, I am sure I have not". The witness had then asked where Guy was and the lad had said that he had left Guy still eating his dinner in the same room as the gun. He had gone out to feed the turkeys and had heard the report from a gun coming from the house. William had said that he was too scared to go into the house and so had called a neighbour and he had gone in. George also informed the hearing that it was William who had come up with the story of the travelling show and then went on to tell the

29. The Green Dragon, Four Crosses.

court of his travels to Brewood and the events leading to the discovery of the corpse.

Under questioning as to why he had not discovered the body sooner he said that the brewhouse had been searched the first day and nothing had been found. There were no signs of blood or shot marks anywhere, but it had been dark in the room and it had only been lit with a candle which he carried. When they had returned from the brewhouse George had once more questioned William, but he still kept to the same story. Later that night he had intended to question William again, but when he went to the bedroom his son was fast asleep.

Questioned in detail about the gun George said that it was the only one he possessed and was always kept on hooks in the back kitchen. The cartridges were always kept separate from the gun in a drawer in the bar. The drawer was not locked, but the bar itself was always locked up. They were No. 5 and 6 cartridges and as far as he knew none were missing. As to the reason why he had not thought it had been fired on the day of the supposed murder he admitted that he used the gun infrequently, the last time being about three weeks previously, and he often forgot to clean it. He remembered that he had used both barrels while out shooting that time and so they would both be dirty. When asked where he had found the gun on his return he reiterated that it was on the hooks, though his neighbours, Nash, Ingram and Adderley, had been in the house and may have put it back there. Finally with regards to the gun he testified that only he ever used it and he had never seen his son, William, use it or even touch it.

In reply to questions about the relationship between the two lads George said that Guy and William were "on good terms: they played together and he had never seen them quarrel or do harm to each other. The little boy would always be with William when they were at home together."

Because it was such a vital point the coroner once more asked about the gun and George testified that "to the best of his knowledge he took the cartridges out of the gun after using it the last time, as that was his rule".

When Matilda Whitehouse gave her evidence she agreed with her husband's testimony, merely adding that she had looked on top of the oven in the brewhouse on the Thursday night but found nothing. However, it was dark in the room. Her only significant disagreement with George's evidence was in regard to the relationship between the two boys. She said that William and her son were in the habit of quarrelling and Guy had complained of William "beating" him. The last time she had spoken to William about his behaviour was five weeks ago. The quarrels were usually over their work around the public house and gardens, jobs set them by their father. However, she could not remember any quarrel on the Thursday morning. She also denied that there was a bruise on Guy's face when she left home that day.

When questioned about the quarrels she said that they were merely the type boys often had over work and she had never heard William "threaten" Guy (she probably meant real physical violence by her use of the word "threaten"). As to the gun she was sure that she had never seen William go to the drawer where the cartridges were kept and had never seen him handle the gun.

The next witness was Thomas Adderley, a farmer at Hatherton. He told the hearing that he had passed the Green Dragon at about twelve on the Thursday morning and had seen the deceased running from the garden to the back door of the building. He was laughing and seemed to put something into his pocket. About twenty minutes later he saw William with a paper bag full of corn in his hand and the young lad asked him if he had seen Guy. When he said that he had not William told him that he had heard the sound of a gun going off in the house and was too frightened to go in. The witness had not heard the gun's report himself, but said to the lad, "I should think the boy has been trifling with his dad's gun and done something". William had replied, "No, my dad's gun is empty."

The witness then went into the building and William fetched the gun from the back room. William turned the barrels down and the witness examined them and found that the gun was empty. However, the right hand hammer was down, but knowing very little about guns he could not say whether the gun had been fired recently or not. What he was sure of was that there were no shot marks in the house or any

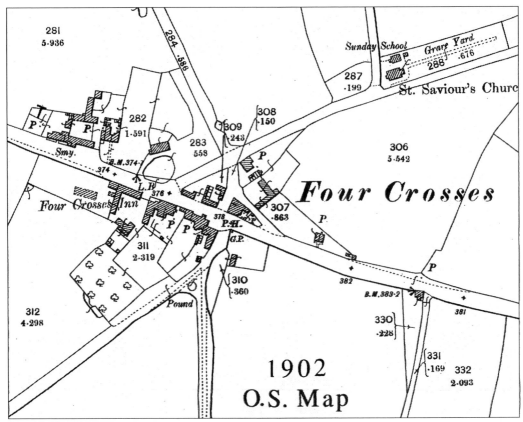

Map 10. Four Crosses.

blood stains and the floors were dry and clean, but he did not go into the brewhouse.

The remainder of his evidence concerned his accompanying George Whitehouse to Brewood and their search of the shows.

John Ingram, also a farmer of Hatherton, testified that on the Thursday morning he had heard a gun report coming from the Green Dragon and five minutes later William had run towards him asking him if he had seen Guy. The lad seemed flustered and said, "There has been someone in the house and I can't find Guy anywhere!" William then went off in another direction. Half an hour later he saw William again and asked about Guy, but William still had not found him. The witness had then suggested to the lad that Guy might have fired his father's gun and, being frightened, had run away. He then asked William to get him the gun so that he might have a look. When he examined it carefully he could find no sign of it being fired recently.

Under questioning from the jury he said that he could see no difference between the two barrels. He was also sure the two lads were always on good terms. Finally, he was certain that it was half an hour between hearing the shot and seeing William.

Ann Hough, who lived near the Green Dragon, was next to give evidence and she said that William had come to her on the Thursday morning and told her that someone had let a gun off in the public house and he could not find his brother. She returned with him and, at his request, she searched the lower part of the building with him. The brewhouse doors were wide open and they searched there also, but could not find Guy. William had then suggested that Guy might be with the van people, but rather strangely added, "Do you think they'll hang me for it?" Afterwards he said, "If those van people have done it and put him away somewhere do you think they will blame me?" She had replied that if Guy was found in the house they might blame him, to which William had replied, "If he is shot I wish they had shot me instead."

Under questioning from the jury Ann was certain that there was no sign of blood in the house or no sign of the floor having just been washed. The brewhouse was "perfectly clean and dry" also.

Jonah Hough, Ann's husband, testified that he had gone to the Green Dragon on the Thursday evening and had asked William if Guy was still missing. William said, "I left him in the house having his dinner while I fed the turkeys and I heard the report from a gun. I ran to the front door and the passage was full of smoke. I went upstairs and could not find him." The witness had then asked if William had looked on top of the oven in the brewhouse and William replied that he had. The witness then suggested that if anyone had done anything to Guy they might have thrown the body in Gailey Pool.

He and William then went towards Gailey Pool with a pike. On the way William had asked the witness if they could blame him if anything had happened to his brother. Once there William searched for the body in the feeder streams of the pool.

Both Ann and her husband told the hearing that as far as they were concerned the two lads "always seemed pretty good friends".

Sergeant Whitehurst, stationed at Brewood, told the court that he had inquired about the boy's whereabouts among the show people on the Thursday and again the following morning, but found nothing. He had returned to the

30. The Whitehouse farm at Four Crosses. Is this where the family moved to after the tragedy or is it a different family?

Green Dragon and with Constable Hall and Mr. Whitehouse had begun a search of the house. The corpse was discovered in the brewhouse on top of the oven, in a sort of recess. It was about six and a half foot from the ground. The body was lying partly on its back with the head towards the front of the oven and the face turned a little to the right. The rest of the body was turned to the left and the legs were tucked up. The lower part of the face was blown away, apparently with a shotgun. The witness immediately sent for Sergeant Upton and a doctor.

Questioned as to why the body was not found earlier the sergeant said that it would be difficult to see in a bad light as it was partly hidden behind some sticks. Only if you looked straight along the flue in a good light was it visible.

Continuing his evidence the sergeant said that he had made a further search of the house the following day and found a loaded cartridge in the closet. It was produced as evidence along with others which had been found in the drawer in the bar.

Doctor Taylor testified that he had carried out the post mortem with Doctor Riley and they had found a quantity of shot in the tongue and adjoining tissue and one shot in the top of the right lung. The body of the lower jaw was missing and the front teeth of the upper jaw were broken off. All the large vessels on each side of the windpipe were damaged and perforated. The witness believed that the lad was shot where he was found and at the time the gun was within three feet of him. He believed that the victim's face was turned straight towards the gun's muzzle when the shot was fired as the entire shot seemed to have hit the lower jaw and the upper part of the neck. That would account for no bone or flesh being blown on to the walls or about the place. The bulk of the blood accumulated in the chest cavity and therefore did not spread around. Death would have been instantaneous and caused by shock and haemorrhage from the shot wound.

Finally he added that they had also found "a trifling abrasion on the left temple which must have been there at least two days, but there were no other marks on the body".

The final witness was Sergeant Upton

stationed at Cannock. He stated that he had first seen William Whitehouse when he arrived at the police station at one o'clock on Friday August 21st looking for the doctor. He accompanied the doctor and the lad back to the Green Dragon and after viewing the body interviewed William as he was probably the only one at the public house when the crime was committed. The lad gave exactly the same account of the incident as he had done to other people.

31. Hatherton Lane in winter.

On searching the grounds around the house the witness discovered a cartridge in the parsnip patch which was a 16 bore and the one produced in evidence in court. He also re-examined the oven and found a tooth and a piece of flesh and bone sticking to the wall about two feet above the flue. On the following day he had the privy seat removed and found a loaded cartridge. It was at that point that he decided to arrest the accused.

Sergeant Upton then went on to tell the inquest jury how the accused had changed his story while in custody. He said that early on the Sunday morning Constable Jackson was on duty when he overheard the prisoner crying and called the witness to see what was the matter. The witness went to the prisoner's cell and

overheard the accused crying and knocking loudly on the cell door. When asked what was wrong the accused had said that he wanted to change his statement. Once cautioned by the sergeant William began. He said that he and Guy had gone into the house to have dinner and afterwards he was going outside when the deceased popped his head up from the top of the oven having hidden there. The accused then took down his father's gun and said, "Now I can see you." He pulled up the right hammer and pointed the gun at the deceased and pulled the trigger. To his amazement the gun went off and he dropped it. He then opened the breach and found an empty cartridge in the right side and a full one in the left barrel. He took them out and threw the full one into the closet.

The sergeant said that the accused finished his statement by insisting that he did not know that the gun was loaded and that they had both played with the gun before when their father was out. It had never been loaded before. Finally, he hoped that he would be dealt with leniently as "he did not do it wilfully".

★You will see in a later episode how the same two officers tell almost exactly the same story about a young prisoner wanting to suddenly change his story in the middle of the night. Makes one wonder exactly what went on in that station at night time.

All the evidence heard the jury retired and after a long deliberation they returned a verdict of "Wilful Murder" and recommended that William Whitehouse be detained in Stafford Gaol until his trial.

On Monday August 31st William Whitehouse was brought before the magistrates at Penkridge to determine whether he should go to trial. The presiding magistrates were Lord Hatherton and C. Chetwynd, Esq. William was defended as he was at the inquest by Mr. Aston. Once all the evidence had been heard William was asked if he had anything to say. All that he could mutter was, "Not guilty, your worship, of doing it wilfully, but by accident."

Mr. Aston made an impassioned plea as to his client's behaviour in the incident, pointing out "that there was evidence tendered that was not consistent with the prisoner's own statement that everything pointed to its being an accident". Also there was no motive for murder as "the evidence of the witnesses was that the boys lived on very good terms and that there had been no serious quarrels". On the fatal morning Guy had been seen "running to the house laughing", hardly the behaviour of a lad who was being bullied. Mr. Aston submitted that there was "no ground on which to commit the prisoner on the charge of wilful murder".

However, the bench had made up their minds and Lord Hatherton stated that the prisoner be remanded to await trial at the forthcoming Assizes at Stafford on the charge of "Wilful Murder".

32. St. Saviour's Church, Hatherton where Guy was probably buried, although there is no longer a gravestone there.

That trial began on December 8th, 1891 before Mr. Justice Day and the long wait for the trial showed on the appearance of the young lad who showed visible signs of suffering. He was pale and rather gaunt from all the worry.

Once the proceedings began all the witnesses from the inquest gave their evidence again with only two further people being called. A farm labourer named Wood who had been working in the field near to the Green Dragon on the day in question said that he heard someone crying loudly and upon going to the bottom of the field he saw the prisoner weighing some potatoes. The deceased was minding a pony in the lane over the hedge and was crying. The prisoner had said, "If you don't hold your noise I'll come over the hedge to you." The lads had obviously been quarrelling. However, another witness testified that between nine and ten o'clock he saw the boys and they were on friendly terms.

Once again as at the inquest and at the magistrates court the Defence lawyer, Mr. Plumbtree that time, argued that the Prosecution had not proved their case for wilful murder as they had failed to find any motive for the crime because both lads were on friendly terms. He argued that the killing of young Guy was nothing more than a tragic accident.

The judge in his summing up dwelt on "the reprehensible manner of the prisoner" in his actions after the shooting. He said, "Supposing his story of accidentally shooting was correct, his first duty should have been to inform the neighbours and render assistance". Instead the prisoner had told a series of lies and he, the judge, thought it should be the duty of the jury to return a verdict of wilful murder or manslaughter.

The jury, after deliberating for about fifteen minutes, returned their verdict of "Not Guilty" and William Whitehouse was set free.

*Of the many cases I have encountered over the years of writing murder stories this is one of the very few where the jury went against the advice of the judge which gives credence to our system of justice. Without that possibility we might just as well have no jury and simply let a judge decide the issue – dangerous move if it ever came about because even judges can make mistakes or be biased.

Postscript:- Probably because of all the notoriety caused by the case William Whitehouse emigrated to America years later, but eventually returned and settled in Newhall Street, Cannock where he died.

DRINK DRIVING?
Hazel Slade/Hednesford 1896

Over the years readers may have heard many stories about animals looking after their masters, guarding them with their lives and even remaining by their side after an accident. Dogs especially seem to be faithful to the end. Remember the story of Greyfriars Bobby, a dandy dinmont, who stayed at his master's graveside in Greyfriars Churchyard, Edinburgh until he died himself. He became so much of a legend that a statue now appears in his honour. Delivery horses are rumoured get to know their daily route or round so well that they have been known to guide even the most drunken man home safely at the end of the day. So was that the case in August, 1896 when John Stanworth and his horse trotted along the Rugeley Road one evening?

John, a milk seller from Hazel Slade, had been in the Uxbridge Arms on Bank Holiday Monday, August 3rd and had promised to take some of the customers home in his cart to Bradbury Lane. At about half past five they all boarded the cart and John set off along the Rugeley Road. Meanwhile, because it was a pleasant evening, Mrs. Sirdifield had decided to take her two young children out to play on the grass wasteland almost opposite her home and possibly meet their father after he had finished work at Bumstead's Foundry nearby. As the eldest lad played neither he nor his mother noticed the cart approaching.

John in the meantime had reached the junction of the Rawnsley Road and the Rugeley Road, opposite to where the young family sat when suddenly the horse lurched to head towards Hazel Slade, its usual route. In an attempt to correct the horse and keep it heading along the same road John must have pulled on the reins severely and the horse panicked. Rather

than keeping it going in a straight line the horse shied and bolted across the grass verge where Mrs. Sirdifield and her two children were. In the mayhem that followed three and a half year old Edward was run over by the cart and his mother was knocked to one side, falling across her baby.

Onlookers rushed to help and mother and children were taken home. Curiously the occupants of the cart merely picked themselves up and walked off in the direction of Bradbury Lane. Even stranger was the action of John Stanworth - instead of staying around to see if anything could be done for mother and children he simply turned his horse and cart and headed home towards Hazel Slade.

Sadly young Edward did not survive the accident, despite being rushed to the doctor and so the police were sent to interview John. Unfortunately for him when they arrived at his home he was in the cowshed and decidedly the worse for drink. Told of the dreadful results of the collision all that John could say was that it was "a bad job". Sergeant Burgess had no option but to arrest him and charge him with causing the death of Edward Sirdifield.

The case and John's possible punishment would depend on his condition at the time of the tragedy. Was he drunk when the incident happened or had he had a few drinks to calm his nerves when he arrived home?

The inquest opened at the West Cannock Inn on the afternoon of Wednesday August 5th before Mr. Morgan. Mr. Coltman, station master at Hednesford, was the foreman of the jury.

Israel Sirdifield was the first to give evidence. He said that he was a labourer at Bumstead and Chandler's Foundry and lived at Lindleys Buildings on Rugeley Road. He had identified the body of his son who was almost four years

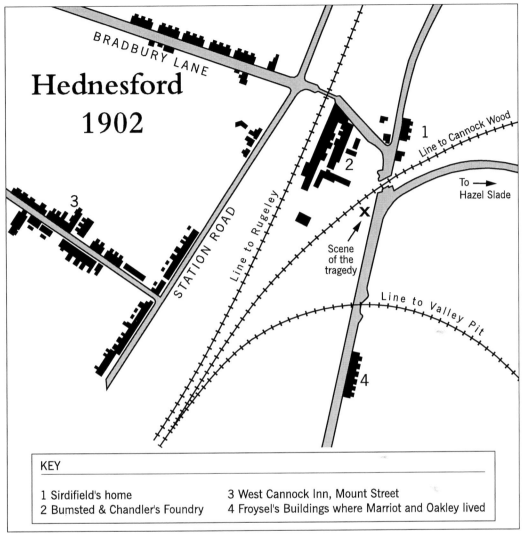

Hednesford 1902

Line to Cannock Wood

1

2

To →
Hazel Slade

3

STATION ROAD

Line to Rugeley

X
Scene
of the
tragedy

Line to Valley Pit

4

KEY

1 Sirdifield's home
2 Bumsted & Chandler's Foundry

3 West Cannock Inn, Mount Street
4 Froysel's Buildings where Marriot and Oakley lived

Map 11.

old. He stated that he was at work on the fatal day and at 5.30 p.m. his brother had arrived to tell him of the tragedy and that if he wanted to see his son alive he must go home immediately. When he got there his son had already been taken to the doctor's and so he went to the police. When he returned with Sergeant Burgess his son was dead.

He also told the hearing that close to his home was a triangular piece of grassland which was slightly raised up from the road. His wife and children often went there to play. Talking of his wife he said that she was still very ill and could possibly die. Sergeant Burgess had told him that the doctor had said that she was so ill that there

was "very little hope of her recovery" and so the sergeant had planned to take her dying deposition.

George Edward Sirdifield of Prince Albert Street, Hednesford, a cordwainer, stated that he was the grandfather and he was with his daughter-in-law and children when the incident happened. He had been and got some sweets for the children and when he arrived back it was all he could do to get out of the way of the horse and cart himself. He had been knocked over by the horse which came up on to the grass. For a moment he was insensible, but when he came round he saw that his grandson was "dead" and the mother and other child injured. He never saw the trap coming.

33. Israel and Naomi Sirdifield c.1910. They had four more children (three boys and a girl) after the tragedy.

Doctor Phillips testified that the child was brought to his surgery at Hednesford at a few minutes past six, but he realised at once that the child was dead. He made an examination and found that several ribs on the right side were fractured and that there was a slanting bruise over the right half of the chest. Later when he performed the post mortem he found that five ribs had been fractured and there was a laceration of the right lung which had been punctured by the fractured ribs. There were no injuries to the head or anywhere else. Death was caused by syncope (a faint which cuts off oxygen to the brain), the result of internal haemorrhage. In the doctor's opinion the young lad had been lying on his side when the cart ran over him.

There then came various witnesses who saw the "accident". John Causer, a miner from Rugeley Road, said that he was sitting opposite the place where the accident happened. He noticed the woman, children and old man sitting on the wasteland with their backs towards the Rawnsley Road. He heard a shout first and turned and saw the child lying in the road close to the side of the turf. He ran and picked the child up. The trap was partly on the road and partly on the green. A man named John

Stanworth was in the trap and he was trying to get out. However, he did not see what happened afterwards as he ran off to take the child home. Mr. Stacey who was close by took him to the doctor's.

When questioned he said that the child was still alive when he picked him up, but died before he got him to the surgery. As to the road he said it was busy with traps that day as it was a Bank Holiday. However, he did not actually see the incident until it had happened. There were several people in the trap apart from Mr. Stanworth.

Samuel Ashley, a miner living in Station Road, Hednesford said that he was about 250 yards away from the scene when he heard a scream. He turned and ran back and discovered the woman on the grass with a baby in her arms. There was a trap standing in the road and everyone had got out except Mr. Stanworth. The witness asked Mr. Stanworth why he did not go for the doctor, but he did not reply. Samuel thought that the driver was drunk. After staying around for about five minutes Stanworth then drove off up the Rawnsley Road.

When questioned as to Stanworth's condition Samuel testified that he reeled about in the trap and he had noticed that he could not sit up straight when he had passed him before the incident. After he had spoken to him about going for a doctor the witness noticed the accused reel backwards and he would have fallen if it had not been for holding the reins.

Obviously the inquest was getting to the crux of the matter at that point, but the coroner decided to adjourn until a future date; firstly, because more evidence would be needed to prove Stanworth's condition on the fatal day; and secondly, to give Mrs. Sirdifield chance to possibly recover and give her evidence.

*In a point of law, if John Stanworth was proved to be under the influence he could be tried for manslaughter, but if he were sober then the judgement would be accidental death unless his driving, even when sober, was reckless.

When the second inquest opened at the West Cannock Inn on Thursday August 20th that was the prime consideration of the coroner and jury. Therefore, Samuel Ashley was questioned further about his previous allegation. Having had time to think it over he began to change his story somewhat. At the new inquest he stated that he would not say that the driver reeled in the trap when it had the people in it, all he would say was that "he had got a red face and that made him say that he was happy". He saw the man after the accident and he seemed "put about", but turned his horse "all right" and went up the Rawnsley Road. His idea that Stanworth was drunk came from the fact that he did not speak and reeled. He said at the time that Stanworth was drunk, but that was not in his presence.

After that new witnesses were called to give their account of the tragedy. Edward Marriot, a miner living on the Rugeley Road, stated that he was in his garden on the evening and saw Stanworth go past at about twenty minutes to six. The witness's friend, Mr. Oakley, stood nearby and said, "That man is drunk," meaning the driver. The witness replied, "Yes, I think the man with a party like that has had sufficient." Not long after he heard a crash and turned to see that someone was run over. He and Oakley ran to the scene and saw the woman and baby lying on the grass in great pain. Oakley then guided the woman and baby home.

*Marriot's garden was one of the allotment gardens opposite the Froysel Buildings on the other side of the Rugeley Road (a football pitch today) and on the same side where Naomi and her children were sitting.

Like Ashley he also asked Stanworth why he did not go for a doctor and got no reply. He believed Stanworth was drunk because when he tried to get up he fell backwards, but the reins saved him from falling. Asked by a juryman if the horse might have jerked the trap to make the driver fall Edward said that it stood "quite still". Asked by another why he thought the driver was drunk Edward said it was because of the way he drove the trap when it passed himself and his friend.

Samuel Oakley, a bricklayer living in Mount Street, Hednesford, corroborated the evidence given by Marriot and when asked about Stanworth's condition he stated that he thought the man was "the worse for beer" while driving along the road. Also when he was in the trap he "stumbled" which made the witness think he

was drunk. However, he could not say whether Stanworth was capable of driving or not, but he did sway to and fro. The trap was only going at a slow trot.

34. Bridge over Rugeley Road. Tragedy happened just below it on the grass verge. The trains ran between Hednesford and Cannock Wood Pit.

James Stacey, an undertaker living at West Hill, Hednesford, stated that he was driving along the road and was about 60 or 70 yards further along the road when he heard screams. He pulled up and saw a horse and trap on the grass and several women either tumbling or getting out of the trap. He left his horses and ran back to find a boy nearly killed. The child was carried home and then immediately brought back out and he took the boy to Dr. Phillips's surgery.

When questioned he said that as he approached the trap along the Rugeley Road the driver pulled out and he passed between the trap and the grass. However, he could not say whether Stanworth was sober or not.

T.C. Longstaff, bank clerk at Willenhall, said that he saw Stanworth near the Public Rooms on Rugeley Road driving with a lot of passengers in his trap. He was driving fast and leaning over the splash board in front. He had the reins in one hand and the whip in the other and was striking the horse as he went. However, he could not swear that the driver was drunk as he was several yards away.

Hutchinson Curry Longstaff, overman at Cannock and Rugeley Colliery, said that he lived on the Rugeley Road about 100 yards from the junction of the two roads. He noticed people going towards the accident and followed them. There he met with Stanworth, whom he had known for ten to twelve years, and asked him to go for a doctor, but he just grunted. After a few minutes the accused drove under the bridge and then turned his horse and drove towards Hazel Slade. He could not say if Stanworth was drunk or not.

Sergeant Burgess told the hearing that after visiting the Sirdifield family at their home and seeing the dead child he went to John Stanworth's home in Hazel Slade. There he found him drunk and leaning against the cowshed door talking to a man. Having arrested him on suspicion of causing the death of the child he took him to Hednesford Police Station. The sergeant said that on the way there the accused staggered against him several times and as they neared the grass where the incident happened Stanworth said. "I did not run over them wilfully". The witness replied, "If you had done that it would have been a case of wilful murder. You're drunk." The accused then said, "I know I had a glass or two, but I knew what I was doing. I wanted to go up Bradbury Lane and the horse became very stupid and wanted to turn up the Rawnsley Road."

The evidence seemed to be stacking up against John Stanworth, but there were those who would testify that he was sober. Robert Henry Blake, coachman at Hednesford Vicarage, stated that he was with Stanworth on the Bank Holiday from twelve o'clock till three thirty and at that time he was "perfectly sober". Stanworth had had one pint in the Hazel Slade Inn, part of which he gave away, and then they had gone to Brereton to deliver a cow.

Mary Ann Kelsey who lived at 7 Uxbridge Street said that she saw the accused shortly before four o'clock near the Uxbridge Arms and from the way that he was talking he was perfectly sober. Robert Bradnick, a watchmaker from Cannock Road, Hednesford said that he saw Stanworth at the bar in the Uxbridge and noticed him purchase two penny worth of whiskey which he drank with some bread and cheese. He stayed with him until about five o'clock and during that whole time he only had a sup of porter out of a glass bought for him by another customer, purely as a thank you. When he left him he was perfectly sober and before he left he overheard Stanworth offer some people a lift home. William Ormson, manager of the Uxbridge, said that he saw the accused in the pub between four and five and only witnessed him having a taste of porter. He was sober and quite capable of taking care of his horse. He had even refused to drink with a man named Rogers.

That man, William Rogers, a miner from Bloxwich, told the hearing that he met Stanworth in the pub and he was sober. Stanworth had told him that he had to go to the witness's brother's home to collect some chickens and offered him a lift there. Seven of them wanted to go to Bradbury Lane and they all got into the trap. The accused drove carefully and when they reached the junction the horse swerved to go up Rawnsley Road. Stanworth tried to pull up, leaning straight back to do so, but the horse made a "bit of a spring" and that pulled the cart across the grass, running over the people there. In his opinion the incident was a pure accident and the accused did all he could to prevent it.

Enoch Cooper, a miner from 6 Bradbury Lane, said that he was also in the trap and Stanworth was sober and drove very carefully. The accident happened exactly as the last witness had described and the driver could not be accused of carelessness. Betsy Rogers of Station Road, Hednesford corroborated that evidence as did Martha and Arthur Bates and John and Arthur Rogers, all passengers in the trap.

We might expect the passengers to take sides with their host, but there were others who would testify to John's sober condition. William Langley, a miner from Hazel Slade, said that he saw Stanworth at home between six and seven o'clock and to his mind he was "perfectly sober". He was of that opinion because he had watched him take his trap through the gate, which was a tight fit, without any trouble. He had known the accused for 14 or 15 years and had never known him to be drunk. Thomas Middleton, also a miner from Hazel Slade, said he lived near the accused and was talking to him when the police officer arrived. While he was talking to him Stanworth had taken the horse from the trap, put his trap away and milked a cow. He thought the accused was sober; in fact he did not think that he had had anything to drink at all from his manner and conversation.

All the evidence heard the coroner instructed

the jury to consider their possible options. There was no doubt that Stanworth had caused the death of young Edward Sirdifield, but in what circumstances. Was the death the result of an accident, "pure and simple", or was it the result of negligence or was it caused by his reckless and careless driving? If they came to the latter conclusion then their verdict should be one of manslaughter.

He pointed out that some twelve or thirteen witnesses had testified to Stanworth being sober and that he thought it quite possible for the excited state of the defendant after the accident "to create a wrong impression as to his condition". The jury, after only five minutes deliberation, returned a verdict of "Accidental Death" with a recommendation that something be done about the piece of grassland to make it safer for people to use.

★Mrs. Sirdifield was still too ill to attend that second inquest, but eventually she would attend the magistrates hearing. Despite his acquittal at the coroner's court John Stanworth was still placed on bail until she could attend a hearing.

35. Naomi and granddaughter, Mavis, taken about 1929 in Huntington Terrace Road.

That hearing finally took place at Cannock Petty Sessions on Monday October 26th before the magistrates, including Lord Hatherton. Naomi Sirdifield at last appeared and she was able to move with comparative ease, though doubts had been expressed as to her ultimate recovery. It was thought that she could remain a cripple for the rest of her life. Her long illness

and fight for life after the tragedy and her condition in court made her the key witness for the Prosecution and she was called almost immediately.

Naomi stated that she was sitting on the grass about two yards from the edge with her youngest son, Richard, on her lap and the older boy lying nearby. At about 5.30 p.m. she noticed a trap coming under the first bridge from Hednesford with several people in it. The next thing she noticed was the horse's foot on her dress and then she was turned right over on to the baby. She got up and ran to the other side of the grass, but then collapsed and became unconscious. When she recovered she learnt that one of her children was dead and the other injured.

At that point Naomi became very emotional, but managed to recover and continue. She said that she did not recognise the driver, but remembered that she had called out to the women in the trap, but they did not offer her any assistance. Finally she said that she was ill in bed for six weeks, but had nearly recovered and so had the baby.

After her evidence the court again heard all the previous witnesses from the inquest, but the Prosecution had managed to find others who would testify to seeing John Stanworth drunk on the fatal day. Mary Ann Speake from Hazel Slade said that on the night in question she was walking down the road when she met the accused driving his trap. He had hold of the reins and was leaning down and swaying to and fro. She was sorry to see him like that as he was always known to be a sober man.

William Price, also from Hazel Slade, said that he saw the accused a few yards from his home on the night. He appeared to the witness to be "entirely helpless" so much so that he stopped to look at him because he was not usually drunk. Hannah Jones from Hazel Slade also said that she met John Stanworth in his trap on that night and he was leaning over to one side. However, she could not say what was the matter with him.

So was John Stanworth drunk or sober before the incident? Lord Hatherton in his summing up stressed that the accused had been in the Uxbridge Arms for over an hour and the witnesses who testified that he was sober were obviously his "boon companions" who had also been drinking. Most of those who said that he was drunk were those who had not been drinking themselves. He, therefore, had no option but to send John Stanworth to the Stafford Assize Court.

*This is one of the rare cases where the coroner and magistrates disagree and unfortunately for John Stanworth the magistrates' judgement took preference.

That court met on December 3rd, 1896 before Commissioner Mr. J. Darling and after hearing all the evidence the jury found him "Guilty of Manslaughter", but recommended him to mercy on account of his previous good conduct. The judge said that he was in no doubt that the prisoner "regretted as deeply as anyone that he had disgraced himself on that day in August, after so many years of exemplary conduct". The jury had added a statement to their verdict, the judge said, that they believed the prisoner was "in an intoxicated condition", but had they told him that they believed him to be sober at the time the sentence would be far more severe. Bearing in mind that that was the only occasion the prisoner was said to be drunk then he would pass a lenient sentence. John Stanworth was given one month's hard labour.

So much for the myth that Victorian courts were always harsh on their prisoners.

Footnote:- Naomi did survive the incident and went on to raise a family of four boys and a girl, having Polly just a year after the affair. However, tragic fate had not finished with the happy family. Isreal was himself knocked down and killed in November 1924. The family had moved to 425 Rawnsley Road, Hednesford probably to escape the memory of the incident on the Rugeley Road and Isreal had since then become a miner.

Just before six o'clock on Saturday November 15th the bus from Rawnsley to Hednesford was coming down the hill towards the Trafalgar Inn when the driver spotted a man walking in the middle of the road. He sounded his horn, but the man only moved when the bus was almost on top of him. The driver moved to the right to miss the man, but he went to the right also. The driver then swerved to the left, but the man did

the same. Unfortunately as the bus passed by it caught the pedestrian with its offside mudguard and he was thrown to the ground hitting his head badly on the roadway. Isreal Sirdifield was taken to a nearby shop and then rushed to the Hednesford Accident Home just along the road. Unfortunately the injury to the head was severe and Isreal died at about one o'clock the following morning.

The inquest was held at the Accident Home on the Tuesday before Mr. S.W. Morgan, nephew of the coroner at the 1896 inquest. Isreal's son, Edward, had identified his father's body and told of bizarre circumstances which might have led to the accident. Apparently his father had had a heavy cold and had used a piece of cotton wool in his left ear which might have affected his hearing. He also had slightly affected eyesight. The driver and passengers told of the man apparently not being aware of the bus until it was almost on top of him and then it being too late. The driver was exonerated and the verdict given was one of "Accidental Death" due to fatal hesitation.

36. Naomi tending Israel's grave at St. Peter's Churchyard, Hednesford c.1925.

Despite yet another tragic setback Naomi carried on eventually dying on December 20th, 1930, aged 62.

*You may have spotted that Edward Sirdifield identified his father's body. Surely Edward died in the accident on the Rugeley Road in 1896? Unlike today it was very common to name a new born child after one that had already died. Victorians saw nothing morbid in doing that. However, it is something like that which can make tracing your family history somewhat difficult.

AN ENGLISHMAN'S HOME
Heath Hayes/Hednesford 1877 - 1879

Just inside the entrance to St. Peter's Church, Hednesford lies the gravestone of Constable Harry Cooke. It reads:-

> To the sacred memory of
>
> HARRY COOKE
>
> First Class Constable in the Staffordshire Constabulary formerly for 12 years trooper in Her Majesty's Second Life Guards who died at Hednesford on the 8th March, 1879 from violence received on duty.
>
> Erected by the inhabitants of Hednesford and brother officers for the love and esteem in which he was held.

37. P.C. Cooke's gravestone at St. Peter's Church, Hednesford.

The incident which led to the death of Constable Cooke began two years before in June, 1877 when a mass meeting of miners gathered in Cannock to hear Mr. Macdonald, their representative in the Midlands, speak. Like meetings before it concerned matters such as the poor wages of the men and the constant laying off of the workers during the summer months, due to the seasonal decrease in the need for coal.

At first all went well, but as tempers grew violence broke out in the crowd and the police had to step in to calm the situation. Unfortunately that angered several of the protesters and scuffles broke out in which two police constables, Williams and Potter, were injured. Two of the miners were arrested and fined £12 and £15 respectively a fortnight later, but a third, Reuben Smith, evaded capture.

Having ascertained that he lived at Heath Hayes the police were determined to bring him to justice and so on the evening of Wednesday June 20th, 1877, concerned that further violence would no doubt ensue during the arrest, Sergeant Kavanagh and five constables made their way to his home. Strangely they were all dressed in plain clothes, probably to avoid detection and not give Smith chance to abscond again. That decision was to prove disastrous.

Arriving at about half past ten at the houses where Smith was believed to be living they found most of the buildings in darkness. Unfortunately they appear to have decided on the wrong house, going instead to that of one Thomas Hyden. Two officers were sent to the back of one of the houses where there was a light while the remainder surrounded the area. Several officers then went to the front door of the house and knocked, but received no reply. They knocked again and the door partly opened, but was immediately slammed shut. One of the officers then lifted the latch and opened the door.

*In the officers' defence it must be made clear that Heath Hayes, like many newly developing mining areas at the time, was nothing more than a series of houses with no street names. 33 year old Hyden, a coal miner, was simply registered as living at No. 20 Heath Hayes. I still have to locate exactly where Reuben Smith lived as he does not appear on either the 1871 Census or the 1881 one, but it was believed that he lived next door to Hyden.

Facing them was a man named Thomas Haydon (Hyden) with a gun at his shoulder who immediately opened fire hitting Sergeant Kavanagh and Constable Cooke. Kavanagh was hit in the left hand which broke the thumb and seriously damaged the fingers. He also received some shots in his face and body, his waistcoat being badly scared. Constable Cooke, to defend his face, held up his left arm and the gun charge tore open the flesh for about three inches above the elbow. Unfortunately the shot then penetrated his chest by the armpit inflicting a very grave wound. As he fell Constable Cooke cried out that he had been shot and the remainder of the policemen rushed in to arrest Hyden. He fought desperately, striking Kavanagh and Constable Bishop violently with the butt of his gun, but was eventually overpowered.

Cooke was then taken to Mill's beerhouse (later Five Ways Inn) where he was treated by Dr. Weston from Stafford, Mr. Cooper from Hednesford and Mr. Horton from Chasetown, but they were all convinced that he would be

lucky to survive. Sergeant Kavanagh was taken back to the police station at Cannock where he was attended to by Mr. Taylor from Cannock. His injuries were not so serious and was soon back on duty. Superintendent Hill was summoned to the station and told of the events and, having done all that he could for his injured officers, returned to Heath Hayes, along with Sergeant Evans and others to arrest Smith.

Smith was apprehended and taken before the Rugeley magistrates on Thursday June 21st where he was charged with assaulting the two constables at the protest meeting and fined £3 and costs in both assaults or he could face six weeks imprisonment for each assault. Hyden was taken before Mr. B. Gilpin, the magistrate at Cannock, on the Thursday where he was remanded until the following Monday.

At the Cannock Petty Sessions on Monday June 25th Superintendent Hill stated, after being asked by Lord Hatherton about the condition of the two officers, that Constable Cooke was "much better and hopes were entertained of his recovery", but Sergeant Kavanagh "was not so good, his injured hand being greatly inflamed". On the Saturday Hyden was remanded for a further week.

At the same court on July 9th the superintendent, in answer to the magistrate Mr. Briscoe, said that Constable Cooke was "progressing favourably". Several shots had been extracted from the wound, but "it was feared that an abscess was forming in the wounded lung, but it was not thought this would be very dangerous". Strangely there was no mention of the remanded prisoner, Hyden.

For several weeks Cooke's survival was in doubt, but with careful nursing and attention he finally recovered and resumed his police duties. However, he was never fully fit, the injury leaving him with a heart condition and dropsy, and by the end of 1878 his condition deteriorated. Ultimately he died on March 8th, 1879 and Hednesford paid its last respects.

On Tuesday March 11th at 3.30 p.m. his cortege left Hednesford Police Station. First in the procession was a large number of Foresters from court "Rawnsley Rangers" held at the Cross Keys Inn to which he belonged; then came the hearse followed by 50 constables under the command of

Mr. Oswell, Deputy Chief Constable of Staffordshire, together with Superintendent Hill; then came the chief mourners, Mrs. Cooke and Sergeant Cockerill and his wife; and finally a large crowd of tradespeople from Hednesford brought up the rear.

Reverend Bullivant conducted the service at the graveside and afterwards the Foresters filed past the grave either side shaking each other by the hand and dropping a laurel each as they did so. The procession then made its way back to the police station where the Foresters and police officers lined up in double file outside to allow the mourners to pass into the building.

Along the whole route of the procession large numbers of townspeople had assembled, many crying for "Long Harry" as he was known locally. At every house in Station Road the blinds were drawn and the windows half closed, showing how much the deceased was respected. A reporter in the *Walsall Observer* wrote *"Few officers of his rank, in so short a time, have earned so much respect from the officers and comrades and from the people in the district in which they have performed their duty as the deceased. His manly spirit, uprightness and uniform courtesy endeared him to all."*

Pity then that the gravestone of Constable Cooke lies almost forgotten.

So what had happened to Thomas Hyden? It would seem that the magistrates continued to keep him in remand, finally deciding that he should stand trial for the attempted murder of Constable Cooke at the Stafford Winter Assizes. That trial began on November 8th, 1877 before Mr. Justice Manisty. By that time Constable Cooke had recovered enough to appear as a witness against his attacker and gave his evidence along with the other police officers involved in the incident.

Constable George Potter, stationed at Hednesford, told the court that on the evening of Wednesday, June 20th he, along with several other officers, went to Heath Hayes to arrest one Reuben Smith. He went to the house of the prisoner thinking it was where Smith lived. He put his hand on the door latch, but the prisoner opened it from inside. At that point he, the witness, shouted to his colleagues, "Come on, he's

for fighting!" whereon the prisoner immediately shut the door violently.

Constable Cooke then came round from the back of the premises and put his foot against the door and then forced it open. The prisoner immediately fired a gun and Cooke shouted out, "I am shot; go in, sergeant, before he can load again." At that they rushed in and after a struggle arrested the prisoner and took him to Cannock Police Station. Questioned by Mr. Underhill for the Defence Constable Potter admitted that all the officers were in plain clothes and did not knock at the door before opening it. Also the prisoner's wife screamed when the door was opened.

Constable Cooke then told the court that he had been round the back of the houses listening at the windows when he heard the last witness shout that the prisoner was resisting arrest. He ran round to the front of the house and at the direction of Sergeant Kavanagh burst open the door and stepped in. The prisoner was leaning against the back wall with a gun resting on his shoulder and as soon as he saw the witness fired.

Sergeant Kavanagh corroborated the evidence of his constables adding that when the prisoner had been taken to the station and charged with intent to murder the officers he simply replied, "I am guilty of that."

At the close of the evidence Mr. Underhill for the Defence argued that there was no case to go before the jury because Hyden was justified in offering resistance to the persons breaking into his home without any lawful excuse. Mr. Macnamara for the Prosecution argued that it was a question for the jury to decide whether the prisoner had or did not have reasonable grounds for believing that the persons were breaking into his house to commit a felony. If he did not have he was not justified in firing his gun and, therefore, was guilty of attempted murder.

The judge told the court that the case was one of great importance in English Law and did not think "upon the evidence submitted he would be justified in leaving the case to the jury". He continued, "The facts were unusual. Several persons – he would not call them police constables because they were in plain clothes – went in the night to the house of a man who had committed no crime and forced open his door.

They never told the prisoner that they were police constables seeking to execute a warrant, although there was an opportunity to have done so before the gun was fired. There was nothing to show anything like premeditated malice on the part of the prisoner, who had no reason to suppose other than that the persons came into his house for the purpose of committing a felony. Therefore the prisoner was justified in using the violence he had done."

Accordingly he had no option but to discharge Hyden who walked free.

The police had learned a bitter lesson. In their haste to arrest a suspect they had forgotten their duty to the public. Before entering a house or on entering it they should have announced their presence and immediately told the person their reason for being there. This still applies today. The old saying – an Englishman's home is his castle – certainly holds true.

THE DEATH OF SHAKESPEARE
Heath Hayes 1885

Today we would be terrified if someone walked into our local public house carrying a gun, but in nineteenth century England it would be considered normal if the person's occupation depended on them having a weapon. Everyone would know them and nobody would be suspicious or alarmed. They would assume that the gun was unloaded and expect it to be kept out of harm's way. But that could never preclude the curious stranger, the mischievous fool or worse, someone intent on committing crime. Which type of man was it then who was to blame for the fatal shooting at the Five Ways Inn on September 15th, 1885?

Seventy year old John Shakespeare had set off from Norton Canes as usual on the morning of Tuesday September 15th to walk to the Five Ways Inn and have his pint and do some business; he had been a game keeper and since retiring had taken up breaking or training dogs (probably gun dogs). Before he arrived at the inn a group of travelling hawkers, four men and a young lad, had settled themselves down in the tap room to drink the quart of ale which they had obtained from the landlady, but without paying. John Shakespeare arrived shortly after and carried with him his gun which he placed carefully in the corner of the room, announcing to all present that it was loaded. Once settled he sat down by a young man named Pickering and the two set about discussing their business over a drink. As he talked he noticed that one of the travellers, a Francis Donnelley, whom he knew slightly, had picked up the gun, but on seeing him with it John immediately told him to put it back repeating that it was loaded.

All quietened down again and John even settled to speaking to the party of hawkers and actually seemed to be doing business with one of them, one Henry Furnifield, and was writing down something on a piece of paper. Unfortunately curiosity or malice must have taken hold of Donnelley as he took the gun yet again that time pointing it at the old man and others in the public house. Without warning the weapon fired and old John Shakespeare took the full blast in the side of his face. Pandemonium broke out as the old man fell to the floor, clutching his face shouting "You have shot me!" His wound was quickly bandaged, relatives sent for and a doctor summoned. When they arrived he seemed to be recovering from the shock and the wound and even asked to be taken home. However, the doctor insisted on examining him at his surgery and took him there in a trap. He died there shortly after arriving and the police were immediately informed.

Meanwhile Donnelley had left the inn, but the landlady had told William Hulme, a farmer and local handyman, to fetch the police. He arrived at Constable Pallett's home, but the constable was out. However, as he was talking to Mrs. Pallett Donnelley walked by on the other side of the road. Without thinking of danger to herself, she approached Donnelley and arrested him to await her husband's arrival. It must be said that Donnelley made no attempt to get away or cause any trouble, but simply went with her to the station house.

The following afternoon, Wednesday September 16th, four of the hawkers were brought before the magistrates at the Public Rooms in Cannock. (The young lad, thirteen year old Owen Gorman, had been let off due to his age, though he still accompanied them to the court.) There before Mr. B. Gilpin the four were charged - Francis Donnelley with causing the death of John Shakespeare and the other three,

Henry Furnifield, Thomas Phillips and Bartholomew Gorman with being accessories to the fact – and all remanded until the Friday.

But was it murder, manslaughter or just a terrible accident? The case would rest on whether the man knew that the gun was loaded and that it was fired deliberately at the old man. The inquest which began at the Crown Hotel, Cannock on Thursday, September 17th in front of Mr. W. Morgan, the coroner, and a jury, headed by Mr. M. B. Anderson, would have to decide.

The first witness was William Green, son-in-law of John Shakespeare, who lived in Norton Canes. He told the hearing that between two and three o'clock on the Tuesday afternoon he was told of the shooting and went straight away to the Five Ways Inn with a man named Emery. His father-in-law was still sensible when he arrived though the left side of his face was blown away. His face was bound up with a cloth and he had asked to be taken home. However, the witness insisted on calling for a doctor.

While waiting for the doctor to arrive he asked what had happened. His father-in-law told him that he placed the gun in the corner of the tap room and warned everyone present not to touch it as it was loaded. When the witness asked if he thought the gun had been fired on purpose he replied that it must have been as he had warned the men on several occasions not to touch it. When Doctor Taylor arrived the deceased was taken to the surgery.

Thomas Emery, assistant manager of the Conduit Colliery who lived near the Hussey Arms on the Chester Road, testified that he had accompanied William Green to the inn and had written down the deceased's replies to the questions. He then proceeded to read what he had written which could be used as a dying man's last statement, something the Victorians regarded as crucial evidence in a possible murder case. It read, "I told him not to touch the gun as it was loaded. He took it out whilst I was writing. He sat by my side. He fetched the gun and shot me. We had not had any words before." (By "words" John had meant argument or cross words.)

The next witness was Mary Mills, wife of Henry Mills, landlord of the Five Ways Inn. She testified that on the Tuesday afternoon, sometime after one o'clock, four men (the prisoners) and a boy had entered the inn and they called for a quart of ale which they did not pay for. The

38. Five Ways Inn c.1910.

deceased came in shortly after them and set his gun down at the end of the tap room in the corner. He told the men that it was loaded and said, "Don't interfere with it." The deceased seemed to know Donnelley and spoke to him.

Shakespeare was doing some business with a young man named Pickering, but the whole group sat together. While the witness was out of the room her little maid served the men with another quart of ale and Mary had to reprimand her for not getting any money off the men. She remembered that the deceased had asked her if the men had paid for the ale. During their conversation the group of men had "ordered her out of the room three times" and questioned if she were the landlady at all. Despite that behaviour the men did seem friendly enough.

The deceased then ordered a third quart of ale for the group and while the witness was out of the tap room she heard a gun go off. She had immediately said to Hulme, "Shakespeare's gun has gone off," and went back into the tap room. There she discovered that the deceased had been shot in the face and saw blood all over him and his pen. Returning to the other room she asked Hulme to help and fetch a policeman. When she said that Donnelley walked out of the inn.

When questioned Mary Mills said that the men and the deceased seemed friendly and had even gone round the back of the inn to chat or do business. They were still friendly when they returned. At the time of the shot that group were the only ones in the tap room and all of them seemed sober.

As was his right in law Donnelley asked Mary Mills "Wasn't the rifle on the seat where men sit on?" to which she replied, "I am not quite sure of that." Obviously Donnelley was trying to prove that the gun was not placed out of harm's way and his picking it up was only natural as he was trying to put it somewhere more safe and it had gone off accidentally.

Dr. Taylor was next to give evidence. He stated that he arrived at the inn at 3.30p.m. and examined the deceased who was suffering from a serious gun shot wound on the left side of his face and neck. The victim was in an extreme case of collapse and shock through loss of blood and the witness insisted on taking him to the surgery. Unfortunately he died within ten minutes of arriving.

The post mortem which followed showed no external marks of bruising which might suggest a struggle during a disagreement. The left side of the face was completely shattered and the upper and lower jaws were blown away. The neck showed signs of laceration from the shot. The doctor said that in his estimation the deceased had died from loss of blood, relapse and shock produced by the gun-shot wounds.

The final witness was William Hulme who told the hearing that he had been in the Five Ways Inn eating his lunch when Shakespeare and a young man came in and shortly after the prisoner and four others entered. One had got a basket of tools, as though they were tinkers, and asked if there were any jobs to be done. They asked for a quart of ale and sat near the deceased and began to chat.

Hulme then said that he believed it was the prisoner (Donnelley) who first took hold of the gun and the deceased told him not to touch it. He thought the gun was near the fireplace close to Shakespeare. The deceased had taken the gun out of the prisoner's hands and put it back in the same place. It was at that point that the witness left the room to return to his work. About ten minutes to a quarter of an hour later he heard a gun go off and went back into the inn. The landlady had asked him to go to the tap room and see what had happened. After seeing the deceased with blood all over him he was asked to fetch a policeman and so went off for Constable Pallett. While he was talking to Mrs. Pallett the prisoner walked by on the other side of the road and Mrs. Pallett went after him and arrested him. He made no fuss and seemed quite sober.

Under questioning from Superintendent Barrett (the reader will meet him in another episode) Hulme had to admit that he could not be sure that it was Donnelley who picked up the gun the first time, but he was sure that it was Donnelley who had left the tap room straight after the shot.

At that juncture in the hearing the coroner adjourned the inquest until the next Wednesday afternoon at three o'clock. The four prisoners were removed to Cannock Police Station.

At that inquest held on September 23rd again at the Crown Hotel and before Mr. Morgan the

39. Five Ways Corner looking down the main street c.1930.

four prisoners were allowed to give their version of the tragic events. However, before they began the court heard Jonathan Pickering's account of what he thought had happened. A seventeen year old labourer from Cannock Road, Hednesford he told the hearing that he was at the Five Ways Inn on September 15th at about a quarter past two with the deceased when one of the prisoners, Donnelley he thought, was about to take hold of the gun which the deceased had placed in the corner of the tap room on a seat. The deceased pushed the prisoner away telling him not to touch the gun and the prisoner left it alone. However, minutes later the prisoner got up and tried to take the gun again, but again the deceased would not let him have it.

One of the other men, the one with only one arm, had a conversation with John Shakespeare about some potatoes and the deceased whispered to the witness that he thought that they were stolen. He also whispered that they were the men who had broken into the Brereton offices. At that point the deceased went outside with the man and continued his conversation. On returning he told the witness that he had been mistaken about the man and that he was a "civil man". It was then that the witness left the group and went back to work.

Under questioning Pickering said that the deceased had the gun with him when he went outside and there was no quarrel between the deceased and the men. The prisoners had two quarts of ale between them while he was there, but they seemed sober. (Remember a quart is only two pints and there were four of them.)

As was his right in law Donnelley was allowed to ask questions of the witness. He asked if Pickering had seen that it was the deceased who first showed the gun to one of the other prisoners and asked whether he could mend it and whether, after they all sat down together, the man tried to take hold of it and the deceased pushed him away saying, "It isn't broken." Pickering replied that he had not heard that. On being asked about the state of the gun Pickering told the court that he had not heard the deceased tell the men that the gun was loaded, only that they should leave it alone.

The first of the prisoners to give his testimony was Bartholomew Gorman, a tinker and licensed hawker from Newcastle under Lyme. As trade was poor at home he had been on the road and was travelling to Lichfield when he met Donnelley and Furnifield, whom he had met before, in Cannock on Monday September 14th. On the Tuesday they all headed towards Lichfield, having been joined by his young brother, and arrived at the Five Ways Inn in the afternoon. The others went in first, ordered the ale and asked the witness to pay for it which he did. The deceased was already there sitting in a corner with the gun placed behind him.

While the others were talking the witness tried to sell the landlady some potatoes, but she would not buy them and so he bought some tobacco. While he was talking to the landlady the keeper (Shakespeare) and the others went outside to do some business. He joined them and when he finally went back inside into the tap room they were all there sitting together except for the old gentleman (Mr. Hulme) and Pickering. Donnelley was standing with his back to the fire and Furnifield was sitting on the right hand side of the keeper who was writing on a piece of paper. Phillips and the witness's brother sat on the left hand side of the keeper.

Donnelley then took the gun and the witness said, "Put that down or you will do some damage." Gorman insisted that he told Donnelley twice to leave the gun alone. However, Donnelley placed the gun in his left hand and cocked it. He put the gun to the "present" and as soon as the witness saw him do that he threw himself on to Phillip's knees. Immediately the gun fired and when the witness got up he saw that the deceased was shot in the face. Donnelley left the room and the witness told the landlady that the keeper had been shot.

Under questioning he said that had he not fallen on to Phillip's knees he would have been the one shot as he was between Donnelley and the deceased. However, he insisted that he had not heard the deceased say that the gun was loaded and was adamant that there had been no quarrelling between the group and the deceased.

The second prisoner to give evidence was Henry Furnifield, a hawker from Monmore Green, Wolverhampton. He testified that when he, Donnelley and Phillips went into the tap room at Five Ways Inn the deceased and a young man were there. Gorman and his brother followed bringing in some potatoes. The old man's gun was placed in the corner close by where the two sat. Before the deceased went outside with them Donnelley had already caught hold of the gun and been told to put it down. However, the old man had not said that it was loaded, but took the gun off Donnelley and put it back down.

The witness then said that he and the old man had some conversation concerning his missing arm and then he, the deceased and the young man went outside and talked about poachers. When they re-entered the tap room the old man sat down "a little away from his gun" and he sat beside him. The deceased had asked him about his address and had begun to write it down when the gun went off.

When questioned Furnifield said that he did not see how the gun went off, merely heard it. When the old man had been shot he jumped up and shouted "I'm shot!" and then dropped down. The witness thought he had been shot too and pulled a handkerchief out to wipe the blood away saying to Donnelley, "What the ---- are you doing?" However, he too was adamant that all of the party were sober (they had only had eight quarts between the four of them that day, four pints each) and that there had been no quarrelling with the deceased or amongst themselves.

It was then Thomas Phillips's turn to tell his version of the tragedy. He was a tin plate worker from Hanley and had met the others in Cannock.

40. Constable Leslie Littlewood. Born at Burton-upon-Trent in 1900, he joined the Staffordshire Constabulary in 1921, first serving at Park Village, Wolverhampton and then at Featherstone, probably the first stationed officer there. He moved to Heath Hayes in the 1930's and by 1939 was in Cannock as a Detective Constable. He retired in 1949 and died in 1973.

The group had got to the Five Ways Inn around two o'clock and the deceased was already there. Before they had gone outside Donnelley had caught hold of the gun and the deceased had told him that as there was a cap on it he might damage it. Despite the warning Donnelley later picked the gun up, cocked it and it fired. Gorman threw himself across the witness's knees or he might have been the one shot.

When he was questioned he said that he had also told Donnelley to leave the gun alone as the deceased had spoken of the cap on it.

Constable Pallett told the hearing that he had gone to the inn after receiving information about the shooting. There he spoke to John Shakespeare and asked him what had happened. The deceased said, "I told the man not to touch the gun as it was loaded and whilst I was writing at the table he fetched the gun and shot me." He told the constable that they had not quarrelled. It was later that the witness arrested Donnelley and charged him with causing the death of John Shakespeare.

Constable Parsons testified that he had accompanied P.C. Pallett to the inn and found the deceased had been shot. He arrested Donnelley and on the way to the station charged him with the shooting. In reply Donnelley had said, "I'm an Irish boy and I done it. My mate knows nothing about it." He then admitted to taking the rifle out of the corner, putting it to his shoulder and then "let him have it", but he did not know that it was loaded. The constable noticed that his prisoner had had a drink. P.C. Parsons also told the court that he had taken the gun from the scene and noticed that the cap was still on the nipple when he received it.

He then proceeded to read out the statement made by Donnelley after his caution. It read, "On Tuesday morning me and Furnifield and the others went to the Five Ways Inn. We had had six quarts of ale at a house before we went there and had two more quarts when we got there. The deceased and a young man were sitting together and we were talking about mending when the deceased got out his gun and said, "Could you mend that, put a new barrel in." I asked him to let me have a look at the gun and he said, "Let it be."

Gorman then came in with some "tatees" and asked the landlady the weight of them. I then went outside with her and sold her two dozen buttons for three and a half pence. I went back in and Furnifield and the old man went outside. When they came back in, and whilst the deceased was writing, I went over to where the gun was. It was on the settle leaning against the wall. I took it up, but did not know it was loaded. I put it up a little above my elbow when it went off.

I was excited and I went away to a distance of about fifty yards from the house. An old man (Hulme) followed me and we went back together without any resistance. I had never seen the deceased before and never passed no words with him. No man was more sorry than I was myself on account of the accident."

All the evidence heard the coroner instructed the jury that so far as he was concerned there was no evidence to prove that Donnelley had murdered the deceased. If they agreed there was still two courses of action they could take – that of manslaughter or death by misadventure (accidental death.) He then ordered the room to be cleared while they deliberated.

It was while the prisoners were being issued from the room that Donnelley was attacked. As they walked along a passageway a son of the deceased struck Donnelley on the right cheek and "inflicted a nasty wound which appeared to have been done with either a poke or a small stick he was carrying; but no one, although several persons were standing by at the time, appears to have seen how the blow was dealt or with what it was dealt". Donnelley was furious and expressed himself "in terms to that effect", but the commotion was soon quelled when it was announced that the jury had returned. Their verdict was one of "Manslaughter against Francis Donnelley" and he and the other men were removed to the lock-up to await an appearance before the magistrates.

That hearing took place at the Police Court at Cannock on Monday September 28th. Only one new witness appeared, Sarah Harris from Heath Hayes. When questioned by Furnifield she said that she had heard Donnelley say to someone, "Mate, look here, I did not intend to point the gun with the purpose of shooting the old man. I meant to shoot my ---- mate." (Furnifield being the mate referred to).

With no further witnesses or evidence to be heard the Bench discharged Gorman, Phillips and Furnifield, but committed Donnelley to the next Staffordshire Assizes on the charge of wilfully murdering John Shakespeare. Allowed to make a statement, Donnelley once more reiterated his plea that the shooting was of "purely an accidental nature".

On Tuesday November 10th, 1885 at the Autumn Assizes at Stafford the Grand Jury threw out the charge of wilful murder against Donnelley, but tried him on the lesser charge of manslaughter. He was found "Not Guilty" and subsequently set free.

ATTACKED AND LEFT TO DIE
Hednesford 1896

We are always led to believe that in the olden days the elderly were much respected and the thought of any crime against them was unimaginable; they had led their lives and deserved to pass their final days in peace. However, the following episode might change our minds somewhat.

(For those readers who have already purchased my other book *Accident, Manslaughter or Murder?* this story will be familiar, but here the whole story is told and many more details have been discovered.)

Eighty year old Catherine Dooley had seemingly fallen on hard times ever since the death of her husband, Edward, a steeplechase jockey, and eventually had had to rely on parish money to survive.

Edward Henry Dooley had been found dead in Hill Street, Hednesford on the morning of February 22nd, 1870. Apparently he had left home on the Monday evening saying that he was going to Norton Canes. At ten o'clock he called at the Holly Bush Inn for a drink, but they refused to serve him as he was already drunk. It appeared that he then walked all the way to Hednesford and simply went to sleep on the road where he died from exposure. The inquest, presided over by Mr. Morgan, found a verdict of "Found Dead".

After her husband's death Catherine lived on her own at Hill Top, Hednesford and tried to be self sufficient. By the 1871 Census she had a small shop there and grew potatoes in her back yard and had ducks roaming freely around her house and garden. The neighbours, especially their children, took delight in trying to annoy her so much so that in June, 1887 she had reason to take some of them to court. There she charged Joseph Birch (8), John Pitchford (10) and Joseph

Ball (12) with assaulting her.

Because of her lack of "sophistocation" she caused "considerable amusement" when she related her story. She said that the boys went into her "kitchen" garden on June 14th and "got on to her taters" (potatoes). When she asked them to leave they pelted her with stones and it was "on the blessed Sabbath". Mrs. Birch had told the boys to roll over the "taters". When she tried to stop them they also knocked her about dreadfully and threw water over her. They also picked up her ducks and knocked them on the floor.

In their defence one of the mothers said that the supposed "kitchen" garden was an open yard and free to all who lived there (remember the back yards of terraced houses?). She also said that Mrs. Dooley was "a great nuisance as she kept a lot of ducks in the house". However, Mrs. Clews who also lived in the terrace gave evidence to support Mrs. Dooley and the court saw fit to fine each boy 3s 2d.

The *Cannock Advertiser* reporter at the Petty Sessions thought the case rather "amusing" calling Catherine "a little old Irish woman". I wonder if the same reporter was present when her name next came up in court?

Too old to care for herself Catherine had eventually taken up lodgings with Mr. and Mrs. Evans of Moreton Street, Chadsmoor and lived with them for about ten weeks prior to her unfortunate death. As was usual every fortnight Catherine received her 2s 6d parish money and went out to do her shopping, more often than not finishing up in one of the local public houses for a drink. The evening of Saturday, November 14th, 1896 found her drinking in the Anglesey Hotel in Hednesford and by closing time it would seem that she was in need of being taken home. Various people offered and the journey towards Chadsmoor began. However, for poor Catherine it would end in her death. Her body was discovered on Lees Common at the back of West Cannock Colliery No. 3 on November 17th, partly naked and covered in bruises.

At the inquest held at the Anglesey on Wednesday, November 18th before Mr. William Morgan, the district coroner, (the same man who had presided over her husband's untimely death) the police confided in the court that they already had three suspects in custody as a great number of people had come forward with evidence. Those men were Henry Freeman, a 38 year old carpenter from Old Fallow Road, Cannock, Joseph Platt (31) and John Henry Fowler (21), both miners from Bradford Street, High Town.

The first witness to give evidence was Mrs. Evans who stated that she had last seen the deceased between ten and eleven o'clock on the Saturday morning at her home just before she went out to collect her parish money. She was not worried when Catherine had not arrived back that night as sometimes the old lady stayed with friends over night, but on Sunday at 1 p.m. a boy brought a satchel, a pocket handkerchief, an old umbrella and some groceries to her house which she identified as belonging to the deceased. She thought at first that her lodger had asked the lad to carry them for her and so Mrs. Evans expected to see Catherine home soon. However, when a neighbour came in they both noticed that the articles were covered in slush and dirt which was unusual.

Getting worried the witness sent the lad down to Mr. Bradnicks to inquire whether Catherine was there. He arrived back saying that she had not been there, but the lad had found a skirt on his way back in the hedge between West Cannock Offices and High Town Bridge. It was a good skirt when Catherine had left to go out, but the strings were all torn off when the lad brought it back. It was at that point that the witness sent her husband, David Evans, to the police. When he arrived back home he said that he had met a policeman who had told him not to worry as he had seen Catherine in the company of Joe Platt the night previous and she might be at his house in High Town. The witness then tried to get in touch with Platt, but could not and so went to the police station herself where she told the sergeant's wife that she suspected that something had happened to Catherine.

Afterwards she met Joseph Platt herself in High Street as he was coming home from work.

41. The Anglesey Hotel, Hednesford c.1920.

She asked him if he knew anything about the old lady and he denied seeing her. However, when she said that the policeman had seen him with her he changed his story and said, "Oh, yes, I did see her." Asked if he had taken her to his house he said, "No, I left her sitting on the road side with some more men." Asked who they were he said, "It was a broad faced man who kept company with a man named Jones from Burgoyne Street."

Mrs. Evans then told the hearing that she met Platt again at ten o'clock on the Monday evening and questioned him again. He maintained that he had not seen any more of the old lady, but when the witness asked him to accompany her to Lees Common he only went as far as High Town Bridge and then said that he had to go and get a pint as he was shocked by the events. In the company of P.C. Taylor the witness went into Lees Field between ten and eleven o'clock on the Monday evening, but could find nothing of Catherine. After further inquiries she discovered that the deceased had been seen on Hightown Bridge.

The prisoners, who were listening to Mrs. Evans's evidence, were then asked by the coroner if they wished to ask any questions. John Fowler immediately declared that Platt had not left the deceased on the footpad, but had in fact shoved her over the hedge into the field. Told to put his statement into question form (they had been allowed to ask questions not make statements, a legal technicality) he asked Mrs. Evans what Platt had said and she repeated Platt's reply.

The next witness was Dr. R. Holton of Hednesford. He said that he had performed the post mortem and had recognised her as a former patient who once kept a lodging house. Externally the body seemed fairly well nourished, but the face was blood stained and there was a half inch wound through the upper lip. There were several ribs broken on the right side which had caused the breast to be full of blood though the fractures had not punctured the lung. There was a slight abrasion on the right forearm and several marks on both forearms which looked like bruises. There was a bruise about an inch in diameter surrounded by other bruises on the inside of the right thigh.

He told the hearing that in his estimation

death was caused by heart failure brought about by shock and the result of injuries received. That was accelerated by exposure to the cold. When asked about a possible sexual attack he said that he had made a microscopic examination of the body, but "though violation might have been attempted there was no evidence that it had taken place".

P.C. Taylor, stationed at Chadsmoor, stated that on the Saturday evening at about 11.15 p.m. he was on duty at High Town with Sergeant Whitehurst when he heard a noise coming from near the West Cannock Offices. On investigating they found the prisoners with the deceased, apparently helping her along as if she were drunk. When he asked what was wrong Platt said, "It's only Mrs. Dooley. Don't lock her up. We will see her safe home." The witness then told them to pick her up and carry her and to be careful not to drop her. Platt and another man took hold of her and carried her towards her home. The two officers then left the scene.

42. West Cannock Colliery Offices c.1970. They became a saddlery before finally being demolished.

On the Monday, because of information given, the witness saw Platt at a house in Burgoyne Street and asked him where he left Mrs. Dooley on the Saturday night. Platt answered, "I left her in the road," to which the witness replied, "You promised to take her home. Why didn't you?" Platt simply said that he wished he had because it would have "saved all this trouble".

Later that same evening the witness went to Lees Common and searched it, but found nothing. On the following morning, accompanied by Sergeant Whitehurst, they returned to the common and about nine yards from the hedge found a shawl. About 180 yards from that shawl they discovered the body in an old disused tramway cutting to No. 4 Pit. The corpse was lying on its right side "nearly naked, cold and quite dead". Her left boot was about 3 yards away and her stays which were torn lay at the back of the corpse, some two feet away. One of her skirts which was all torn was about two feet away while her dress was also about two feet from the body. Her bonnet with all the strings torn lay one foot away and a string of beads were nearby. The corpse was then removed to the Anglesey Hotel.

The constable then told the court that at about 2.30 p.m. that same day he went to West Cannock No. 4 Pit with the sergeant and arrested Fowler as he came up the pit. Charged with being involved with the death of Catherine Dooley Fowler replied, "I know nothing about it. I never seed her." At about 3.45 p.m. the same afternoon Platt was arrested as he came up the pit and he simply replied, "All right, I will go with you." Once at the police station both men made a statement.

Unusually the coroner allowed Superintendent Barrett, who had attended the hearing on behalf of the police, to question his own constable. P.C. Taylor reaffirmed that he and the sergeant had seen all three men with the deceased on the night in question and, being assured that they would see her home, they had gone on their duties. He also added that the hedge at Lees Common had been broken down and a large gap made about 280 yards from where the body was found. There was evidence of a struggle on the hedge in one part.

Once again the coroner gave the prisoners the opportunity to ask questions. Fowler then asked both Platt and Freeman if he was the one who had thrown the deceased over the hedge, but before they could answer the coroner intervened to warn them that anything they might say could prejudice their future dealings with the police concerning the case. Both then remained silent. The coroner then adjourned the case pending further police investigations. All three men were then taken before the magistrates, Messrs. Wolverson and Evans, and formally remanded until the Petty Sessions at Cannock.

The adjourned inquest began on Thursday, November 26th, once again at the Anglesey Hotel. Henry Freeman had got himself a lawyer, but the other two were unrepresented. Did he have more to fear than the others?

Martha Evans was recalled and gave further evidence of her conversation with the prisoner, Platt, as they tried to find the deceased. She said that he had told her, "If the Lord will only forgive me for this time, if it was my mother I would not put hands on her." Platt was allowed to question Mrs. Evans, but she was adamant that that was what he had said.

P.C. Taylor restated his previous evidence and was questioned by Mr. Lexton, councillor for Freeman, who asked the officer to tell of a meeting with his client on Tuesday, November 17th. The constable then told the inquest that he had seen Freeman in the Anglesey Hotel on that evening and told him that a man named James Lunt had come forward and admitted to seeing the deceased on the Sunday morning in the railway cutting as he was going to work at the West Cannock Wagon Works Yard. Lunt had said that the old lady was "alive and alright" and that he had "picked her up and put her on her feet". (Lexton was implying that his client had nothing to do with the actual death of Mrs. Dooley.)

Questioned further by various jurymen and the coroner the constable said that there was the appearance of a struggle around the body and from the appearance of the clothes in his opinion they had been dragged from her in that spot and not from her being pulled through the hedge. As to possible motive for that happening he stated that "it was common knowledge in the district that the deceased had money". (It was a frequent practise in those days for elderly ladies to sew money into their petticoats for safety. That could explain why all her clothes were torn from her.)

George William Barratt, a surveyor from Brownhills, presented the hearing with a diagram of the places where various items were found scattered around the field. There was a running stream about 2 foot 6 inches wide to cross and a ditch that "would offer difficulties to a drunken old woman to cross". In his opinion it was "impossible for an old woman, 80 years old, to get over those places, especially if she were not sober".

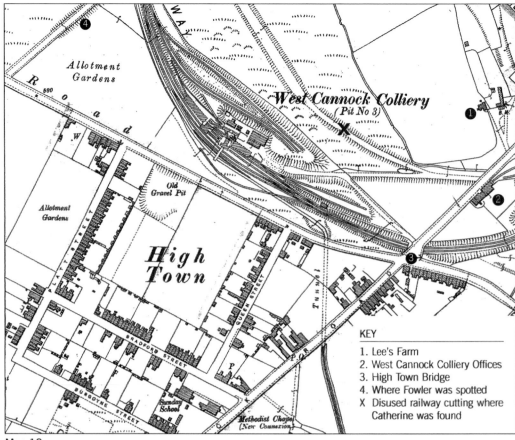

Map 12.

The next witness was Sergeant Whitehurst who corroborated the constable's evidence, but then went on to relate the events after the fatal evening. He told the hearing that he sent to the West Cannock Yard for help and Freeman was among those who carried the corpse away. However, it was his next evidence which was to prove costly for the prisoners.

After arresting Fowler and Platt they made their statements at the Police Station. Platt stated that he had helped carry the old lady as far as the High Town Bridge and then had left her, leaving Fowler and others with her. Fowler stated that after they had met with the policemen Platt and a man named Henry Dowding had carried the deceased up to the bridge and left her there. A man named James Spooner was there, but had soon left. He, Fowler, and Platt were the last to leave the scene and he had then gone home with Platt. He was adamant he had never touched the deceased.

Freeman was arrested on the Tuesday night and he stated that he had not "interfered" with the old lady. He had found her lying down on the Anglesey Drive and assisted her to Udall's Shop where she lay down again. He and a man named Spooner took her as far as the West Cannock Offices where they met the policemen. It was then that he and Spooner walked off as far as John Street where they parted company.

On Wednesday November 18th the sergeant charged the three prisoners and in front of all three read out the various statements already given. That caused immediate disagreement between the prisoners (obviously the sergeant's intention).

The heated debate went as follows:-

Fowler: You did not leave me with her. I went down the road with you.

Platt: Yes, I did.

Fowler: You know you didn't. You can't deny it if you

tell the truth. You couldn't deny it on Sunday when I went in Newell's.

Platt: *I will out with it now and tell the truth. Who was it that pushed the old woman over the hedge when me and the other man were carrying her?*

Fowler: *It's a lie. What are you going to say now.*

Platt: *When we were carrying her you came up and a gave her a shove and pushed her on top of the hedge and said that's the best ---- place for such a varmint as her.*

Fowler: *I went with you! Can you deny this? After we had left her near the bridge didn't you say "Let's go back, Jack, and throw her over the hedge".*

Platt: *I did not!*

Fowler: *I know you did.*

Platt: *What did you say to me in the Jolly Collier on Sunday dinner time. I know what you said. When I asked you what you had done with the old woman you said "Shut up you ---- fool, the old ----'s dead.*

Fowler: *Yes and what did you say to me in the Collier on Sunday afternoon. You said, "Jack, I heard that the old woman was dead and it's the best place for her.*

Platt: *Oh! Go on; try and clear yourself.*

The sergeant told the court that all during that heated argument Freeman did not speak. Finally he stated that while he had charge of Fowler in the Anglesey on the Tuesday Sergeant Burgess had said that a man named Fountain was in the hotel and he had helped carry the deceased and he had been told that Fountain had shoved her over the hedge. (Further confusion for the court.)

The next witness, George Prince, a labourer from Littleworth Road, Hednesford said that on the Saturday night he was coming back from High Town at 11.30 p.m. via the bridge when he heard someone say, "Don't kill me". It was a feeble sounding voice and came from the direction of Lee's Common. He then heard a man say, "Take that you ----" which was followed by the sound of a blow. He saw no one clearly, but did notice a man near No. 3 Pit mound walking towards the railway cutting.

Questioned by Platt Mr. Prince had to admit that he did not recognise the man nor could he say that Platt was there.

Ellen Bradbury from Chadsmoor testified that at about eleven o'clock on the Saturday evening she was going home from Hednesford when she saw some men assisting the deceased along the road. One was Jack Spooner, but she did not know the others. She followed them up to the bridge and they left the deceased there. Two other men, one Joseph Platt, arrived and then the police. When the police left two young men arrived and one said, "Chuck the old ---- over the hedge". The witness then said to the men, "For God's sake don't. You've got a mother of your own somewhere." Spooner then walked home as far as John Street with the witness and her husband.

Fifteen year old Louise Dando who lived with her parents on High Town said she was coming from her uncle's shop in Market Street when she saw two men dragging the deceased towards the High Town Bridge. Platt was one and she thought Freeman the other. She saw both of them throw the deceased into the hedge and when she stuck there they pushed her over it. Being frightened she ran home. There were other men at the scene also.

Fourteen year old William Saunders from Chadsmoor stated that on the Saturday he was going down to the barbers at 11.30 p.m. to get his hair cut when he saw Freeman and two other men trying to get the deceased along the road. Finding the shop shut he returned and as he neared the gate by the West Cannock Offices he heard one man say, "Let's chuck the ---- over the hedge". Two of the men then got hold of the woman, put her on the hedge and then pushed her over. Freeman did not touch the deceased, but the other two jumped over the hedge into the field. Freeman came away with the witness as far as Dando's shop and then the witness ran home.

When questioned young William said that he did not think the men jumped on the deceased though he did see one sit on her.

The court then heard from James Lunt, the young man who supposedly saw Catherine Dooley alive and well on the Sunday. He stated that he was a striker at West Cannock Colliery and lived at Brindley Heath, Hednesford. He told the hearing that he was walking along the railway cutting in Lee's Common on the Sunday morning towards No. 4 Pit when he came across

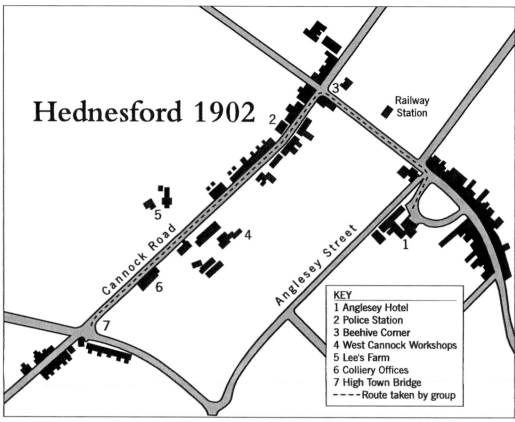

Map 13.

the body of a woman. He was not sure if she was alive or dead, but shouted "Get up!" and then walked on. The next day he saw Freeman in the West Cannock Yard and, having heard that Freeman had been with the woman on the Saturday night, said to him, "Hello, Kitty, how are you going on?" Freeman then admitted trying to get the woman home, but said that he had left her by the bridge.

Lunt then stated that Freeman had seen him the next day and had asked him if he had heard anything about the woman. Freeman then told him that the police had been dragging the brook. Later the same day Freeman approached him again and told him the police had found the body and if they questioned him, the witness, he should say that she had spoken to him on the Sunday morning.

Under cross-examination Lunt said that he did not go near the woman on the Sunday because he thought she was drunk. He bragged to his mates that he had seen a body up the cutting, but

they did not go to look. He had eventually realised it was Kitty Dooley because he had heard that she was missing and that was why he teased Freeman the way that he did.

(Lunt had not realised the importance of his supposed meeting with the deceased. If she were still alive when he saw her he could be implicated in her death.)

George Bates, a labourer living in Burgoyne Street, High Town, testified that on the Sunday he had gone a walk with the prisoner, Platt, near the West Cannock Offices and discovered a skirt. The prisoner had said, "Perhaps it's old Kitty Dooley's" and then went on to tell of the previous night's episode and how he had left the old woman in the road with some other men.

When questioned Bates said that he had been with Platt in the Anglesey on the Saturday night at about 6 o'clock, but left at nine to go home. On the Monday evening Platt had been at the witness's home because they were friends.

Fifteen year old Thomas Davis who worked at

Mr. Maxted's hairdressers in Market Street, Hednesford stated that he was walking home towards High Town at 11.40 p.m. and when he was near Udall's shop he heard a woman squealing. The sound seemed to come from Lee's Common, but not close to the hedge as that was where he walked. However, he saw no one because it was rather foggy.

At that point in the proceedings the coroner stopped the case as he considered the evidence "most unsatisfactory and there was every appearance that evidence had been suppressed". He made special mention of James Lunt's evidence which he considered unsatisfactory for someone who had seen the victim and told his mates about it yet they did nothing. With that in mind he closed the inquest and ordered that another take place on December 10th to give the police time to investigate matters more.

(The coroner knew that the case ought to go before the Assizes because a crime had been committed, but as it stood it would probably be thrown out due to the confusion of evidence, especially as to who had actually assaulted Catherine Dooley and who was present at the time of the assault. Today's police have to be certain of their facts before a case goes to trial just in case the guilty get off on some technicality.)

On Friday, November 27th James Lunt was arrested by Sergeants Whitehurst and Burgess and charged with being an accessory after the fact. He was taken to the police station where he made the following statement:- "At about 8 a.m. on Sunday November 15th I was going from the West Cannock Yard across Lee's Common. I passed through the cutting and saw Mrs. Dooley apparently asleep. I asked her what she was doing there. She replied, "I have a pain in my heart." I lifted her up. She was dressed and had all her clothes on." Despite several warnings as to telling lies Lunt insisted that he was telling the truth and so the police had no option but to take him before the magistrates.

That special session began the next day before Messrs Hamstead, Wolverston and Evans. All four prisoners were present, but the hearing only concerned itself with evidence against Lunt. Edward Millington, a striker at the West Cannock Works, said that on November 15th

Lunt had told him that he had seen a dead body in the cutting of No. 3 Pit, but on being asked to show the witness where it was Lunt had changed the story to say that the woman was not dead but alive. When asked how he knew the person was alive Lunt had said that he had picked her head up and she was well enough to make her way home. He also said that the woman's "bodice was off". Under questioning Millington said that he believed the second version to be the truth.

Two other witnesses who had not come forward at the inquests also gave evidence before the magistrates. Fourteen year old Ada Stokes from Bradford Street, High Town stated that on the Saturday night at 12.15 a.m. she and Sarah Ann Hodgkiss, John Gallier and Thomas Jenkinson were on the footpath leading from Belt Road to the West Cannock Colliery when they met John Fowler coming across the railway line from the direction in which the body was found. She knew Fowler well and he had said, "Don't tell them where I've gone" and then walked away. Under questioning Ada admitted that she was not exactly sure of the time because they did not have

43. Royal George Off Licence, High Town 1924.
Pictured left to right - Mrs Gertrude Allen, Mrs Rose Beard, Mrs Sarah Evans and husband William.

a clock at home, but thought it must have been after midnight as she had been sent on a errand to Dando's shop and found it closed and so had gone to another along the Belt Road.

Fifteen year old Sarah Ann Hodgkiss stated that she was with the previous witness on the Saturday night going on an errand and they had met John Fowler. However, she disagreed with Ada Stokes about being on the footpath leading to the colliery, but said they stayed on the Belt Road all the time.

At the end of that hearing the Clerk began to read out the statement made to the police by Lunt when Mr. Aston, his solicitor from Cannock, objected to it being evidence against his client. Once again the police had to go through how Lunt had made that statement stressing that Lunt had been warned about making false statements. Sergeant Whitehurst, who was present during the statement, added that Mr. Arnott, the colliery manager, who was also present when Lunt said the deceased was "fully clothed", declared, "That cannot be. I saw her skirt on the footpath on the Sunday morning". However, Lunt insisted that she was fully clothed when he saw her alive on the Sunday.

The magistrates had no option but to remand Lunt, along with the other three prisoners, to appear at the next inquest to be held on December 10th at Hednesford.

What on earth made Lunt persist with his story which was obviously far from the truth would never be discovered. Maybe it was his fear of Freeman or perhaps he was just too frightened to admit he had told lies. Whatever the case he appeared in the dock with the other three prisoners at the third inquest.

The hearing began with Superintendent Barrett stating that the police had no further evidence against Lunt and at that point Mr. Morgan read out part of the Act which defined a coroner's jurisdiction. It clearly stated that a coroner only had jurisdiction with prisoners being charged with being an accessory "before" the fact and as Lunt's "crime" was "after the fact" they could not hear his case. His case was to go before the magistrates again to determine if he should go to trial at Stafford.

More witnesses had came forward for the new

hearing. Thomas Jenkinson, a miner from High Town, stated that he was up the railway line near No. 3 Pit on the Saturday night walking with Sarah Ann Hodgkiss towards No. 1 Pit when he saw Fowler going in the direction of Queen Street. He carried on along the footpath with Sarah (Gallier and Stokes were behind them), but saw no one else.

*Thomas Jenkinson appears in another episode in this book when he and his brother, George (see below) attacked Samson Blewitt at Pye Green. That happened in 1900. Perhaps Sarah's parents did not like her keeping company with Jenkinson and that was probably why she would not admit to being off the road with the group.

John Gallier, a miner from Burgoyne Street, told the hearing that he was with Sarah Ann in a gullet (gulley) leading from No. 3 Pit at about 11.20 p.m. when Fowler came up from the direction of High Town Bridge. Ada Stokes had called out to him and Fowler said, "How do, Jack. Platt and another man have just thrown a woman over the hedge." The prisoner then followed the witness and Stokes down Queen Street and then went towards his house.

Frederick Richards, a miner from Burgoyne Street, said that on Sunday November 15th he had gone to the Jolly Collier at about six thirty and shortly after Platt, Freeman and a man named George Baker had come in. All four sat down for a drink and at about seven o'clock Fowler and George Jenkinson entered. The witness overheard Platt say to Fowler, "I wonder how Kitty Dooley went on last night", to which Fowler replied, "Shut up you ---- old fool, the old ----- is dead by now." The two then spoke in whispers after that and the witness left the company at 7.45 p.m.

Just to clarify everything for the jury the coroner recalled Dr. Holton who stated that the victim's ribs were broken, but he did not think that the fall from the hedge would do that unless the whole weight fell in one place. It was quite possible for all the ribs to have been broken by a person sitting or jumping on the deceased and if the foot went down flat on her body then there would be no external marks. When questioned as to the number of attackers needed to cause such injuries he stated that it was quite possible for just one man to carry the deceased over the common as she weighed barely seven stone and for one man to attack her.

Finally the coroner deemed it possible to end the case and began to sum up the evidence. As for James Lunt he said that he had "shown a brutal indifference" to the victim "coupled with a cowardly fear that he might be implicated in some way with this outrage and crime", but he did not think it necessary to say more. As for the three other prisoners it had been well established that they had been with the deceased on the tragic night and the evidence given, though contradictory on occasions, should make it possible to say whether they were responsible for the old lady's death. He went on to say that even if the dreadful deed had been carried out by just one man then from statements made by witnesses the other two knew what had happened.

As to motive he pointed out that the deceased did have money and so robbery was the probable reason for the assault. He then clearly stated that "if persons in pursuit of an unlawful purpose cause the death of a person then it is wilful murder, not manslaughter". It had also been upheld in law that even if only one person caused the death of a victim "all those present with the same objective were principals in the crime". He, therefore, instructed the jury that if they found one man guilty then they must find all three.

After an hour's deliberation the jury returned a verdict of "Wilful Murder" and all three men were committed to trial at Stafford Assizes.

*Most of the jury who had sat patiently through all three inquests were local businessmen. Some of them still have ancestors in the area and still running businesses. They were:-

Mr. Marston, T.J. Witts, T. Griffiths, W.H. Pointon, F.W. Smith, J. Heggs, W. Webster, G.M. Gascomb. A. Catile, R.J. Stokes, A. Maxted, J. Smith, S. Stanton, G. Taylor and lastly T. Brown.

Following the final inquest all four men once again appeared before the magistrates on December 17th with Lord Hatherton presiding and once again the witnesses retold their stories, but there were several new witnesses who came forward. Edward Poole, barman at the Anglesey Hotel, stated that he saw Platt in the taproom on November 14th and he was sober. Not long after he noticed the deceased in the passageway as she was leaving. Freeman, who had been in the smoke room, left at closing time.

William Fountain, a labourer living in Blewitt Street, Green Heath, said that he saw Freeman and the deceased on Station Bridge, Hednesford at about 11.00 p.m. The deceased appeared to be drunk and Freeman was holding her up. She was carrying an umbrella, a satchel and a bundle which the prisoner asked the witness to carry. He agreed as he was going in the same direction, but he had advised Freeman to take the deceased to the police station across the road. The prisoner had refused saying he was going to Chadsmoor and would take her. Fountain also stated that Platt and another man were on the other side of the road near the Beehive.

James Spooner, a miner from John Street, Chadsmoor, said that as he was walking home from Hednesford a young man named Fountain gave him a satchel, an umbrella and a bundle to carry. The deceased fell down on one occasion and Freeman told her to get up as they wanted to get to Chadsmoor. Platt and Freeman walked on either side of the deceased. As they reached the West Cannock Offices the group met the police and the witness carried on walking home. He took the articles home with him, but returned them to Catherine Dooley's lodgings the next day.

All the evidence heard Freeman's and Platt's solicitor, Mr. Loxton, argued that the men should be given bail rather than be detained in prison until the Assizes which were in March as both had families (Freeman had a wife and six

44. Beehive Corner, Hednesford looking along Cannock Road c.1930.

91

children and Platt a wife and one child). However, the magistrates would not agree and Freeman, Platt and Fowler were committed to Stafford Gaol to await trial. That left James Lunt. It was quite obvious that he had told a series of lies which had brought him to court, but the magistrates could find no connection with the death of Catherine and so he was discharged, but only after receiving a severe warning as to his future conduct.

The trial of the three prisoners began on Wednesday, March 10th before Mr. Justice Wright. However, before it got under way Mr. Kettle and Mr. Chateris for the Prosecution stated that they considered the case against Platt to be weak and not worth pursuing and so asked the judge that he might be discharged to enable him to be called as a witness against the other two prisoners. Both judge and jury agreed and Platt was found "Not Guilty".

The case then centred on Henry Freeman, but it quickly became clear that there was little evidence to connect him with the actual attack on the deceased. In fact Ellen Bradbury changed her evidence at the trial and declared that the person whose idea it was to throw the old lady over the hedge was neither Platt or Freeman, but she could not say who actually did say it. Even when questioned by the judge about her first statement that Freeman had made the remark Ellen was adamant that it was not him. All other witnesses testified that they only saw Freeman helping the deceased along the road. With those statements in mind the judge directed the jury to return a verdict of "Not Guilty" in favour of Freeman which they did.

That left John Henry Fowler to face the charges. Witnesses would say that he was seen running away from the scene and he was the one who said that Mrs. Dooley was dead when Platt confronted him in the Jolly Collier. Also he was the one identified as the person who pushed the old lady over the hedge. However, Mr. Kettle had to agree that there was little to prove that Fowler had murdered the woman and a case for "Wilful Murder" would be hard to prove. The judge agreed and directed the jury that if they thought that Fowler's actions had "hastened death" then manslaughter should be their decision.

The jury retired and within a short while they reached their decision - Manslaughter against Catherine Dooley. In passing his sentence of three years penal servitude the judge stated that the sentence was relatively short because the jury had not been given sufficient evidence to prove that he was "party to further violence" on the old woman. Had they had that proof the sentence would have been "a prolonged term".

MEET ME ROUND THE POOL
Hednesford 1919

There are not many events which remain embedded in the folklore and psyche of local history, but ask anyone who has lived in the area for years and they can quickly relate stories that they have heard concerning our ugliest murder. As a teenager in the 1950's I can vividly remember walking through the actual scene of the crime and, being informed of the gruesome details, expecting to find some remnants of the horror. Unfortunately, like the fish that grows each time its catch is retold, this episode is exaggerated and parts added that are totally untrue. Even as I wrote this chapter I was being given "false" information. "After he done her in he sang *At the End of a Perfect Day* in the Uxbridge", my confidant related. Nothing so ironic happened. So what are the facts concerning the Gaskin Murder?

The story began with the marriage of Thomas Henry Gaskin (23) to Elizabeth Talbot (17) on July 20th, 1913 and on October 10th of that year they had a child, though it was not certain if Thomas was the father. At first they lived with Gaskin's mother, Mrs. Harriet Williams (she had been remarried some years before to Henry Williams), then they moved to an "apartment" in St. John's Road, Cannock before finally moving to rented accommodation at Brindley Heath close to Elizabeth's mother at 72.

However, by March of the following year Gaskin had been "removed by the Authorities" to Portland Prison for a series of petty thefts. (He had already served almost a year in Stafford Gaol between 1912 and early 1913 for similar offences.) He stayed there until 1916 and having served part of his sentence was given the option of joining up to fight at the Front. Elizabeth had had another child while he was in prison, born in February, 1916 and so obviously it was not Gaskin's, though

the little girl had died by the June.

It is not clear whether Gaskin found out about the child while in prison, but he joined the Royal Engineers in late 1916 finally going to fight at the Front by May, 1917. He had by then not seen his wife for almost three years, but in the September of 1917 he had his first furlough and rejoined his wife, living at his mother's home, but discovered that Elizabeth had been unfaithful. (Evidence given at the inquests stated that Elizabeth had had two illegitimate children during that time, though her mother hotly

45. Elizabeth Gaskin on the right with neighbour, May Law, who became Mrs Davis of Stafford.

denied the second.) Whatever the truth their relationship was damaged and it was rumoured that he even threatened to kill Elizabeth, having taken his service rifle to her. It had proved to be unloaded, but a sign of what was to come? When he had another furlough in February 1918 the couple were together again and all seemed fine.

However, on his demobilisation in the January of 1919 he discovered that Elizabeth had had another child on January 6th believed to be by a soldier from the Camps named Monty Harris. He determined then that their marriage was over and went to live with his mother in Bridgtown. He got his old job back at West Cannock No. 3 Pit in Hednesford, but on more than one occasion Elizabeth waited for him on the pit bank to discuss maintenance money for her and the children. His answer was always the same - he would give no money and wanted a divorce. But Elizabeth persisted which brings us to the fatal day.

On Wednesday, February 19th Elizabeth received the infamous note which seemed to be to her advantage. It simply read, "Meet me round the Pool. Important." Thinking it was about money or a possible getting together again she quickly put on her coat and went to meet Thomas. She was never to be seen alive again.

On the Thursday morning Mrs. Talbot, fearful of her daughter's whereabouts, travelled to Bridgtown to see Thomas at his mother's home. Once there he told her that, although he had written the note, he had not gone to the proposed meeting. He told Mrs. Talbot that he had intended to tell Elizabeth that he wanted her to stop following him as he wanted a divorce, but had not seen her. However, he promised to meet Mrs. Talbot again that afternoon on Hightown Bridge. She never turned up. Instead she had gone to the police station to report her daughter missing and tell of her fears.

They began an immediate search of the Hednesford area, concentrating on the Rugeley Road and around the Pool (it was by then just a boggy meadow). Officers were drafted in from around the area and searched every bit of the woods surrounding the Rugeley Road. The reservoirs were dragged and police constables even made their way through a long culvert close to the Valley Pit. Certain that Thomas knew

something of his wife's disappearance they interviewed him the same day, but he insisted that he knew nothing saying, "All I can say is I did not see her on Wednesday. That's all I can say."

The search continued on the Friday, but still nothing was found. However, by the afternoon they decided to arrest him. At four o'clock, just as he was about to go down the pit, they detained him and took him to Cannock Police Station. (He asked not to be taken to Hednesford Police Station for some unknown reason.) Despite more questioning he refused to acknowledge that he had seen Elizabeth on the fatal Wednesday, keeping to his story that he had not turned up to the proposed meeting.

On the Saturday afternoon Gaskin was taken before Mr. Thomas Mason, the magistrate, and charged with murdering his wife. He refused to have anything to say regarding the charge and Chief Superintendent Pilliner applied for a remand in custody until the

46. Thomas Henry Gaskin 1917.

following Tuesday. That was granted. The police then continued their search throughout the remainder of Saturday, but still found no body.

For reasons only known to Gaskin himself on Sunday February 23rd he suddenly changed his story. Superintendent Morrey was just about to sit down to his dinner when he received a telephone call from the station. In it Gaskin said, "Can you go to Hednesford and search for the body without the Hednesford Police knowing." Morrey replied that he could and Gaskin continued, "Well, I will take you and show you where it is. You will want two men and two drags to pull in opposite directions."

Gaskin was then taken from Cannock Police Station in a taxi with Superintendent Morrey and Inspector Woolley to Hednesford where he guided them to the Gas Works in Victoria Street. There they had to climb over a five foot wall to reach the gas holders and they discovered the torso of the unfortunate Elizabeth at 4.50 p.m. after dragging the water container surrounding the holder. The torso was taken to the mortuary in the Gas Works where it was briefly examined by Dr. Butter and then removed to the Cannock Mortuary for closer examination. Leaving some police dragging the water Gaskin then took other officers to the plantation next to Pool Pit (today's Valley Road). They entered the wood and he quickly took them to the exact spot where he had killed his wife

By the Monday they had not located the head and large crowds visited the scene to watch as the police continued their dragging of the water around the gas holder. Eventually that was discovered at 9.40 on the morning of Tuesday, February 25th by Constable Baker not long before the inquest was to start.

47. Sidney William Morgan, Staffordshire Coroner.
He was the nephew of Wilfred William Morgan who appears in many of the episodes and was the coroner in Staffordshire from about 1870 until 1910 when Sidney took over.

That initial inquest was held at the Council Offices in Cannock before Mr. S. W. Morgan and large crowds gathered in Market Square hoping to catch a glimpse of Gaskin. Mr. Ernest Lindop was foreman of the jury and the police were represented by Chief Superintendent Pilliner and Superintendent Morrey.

48. Mrs Talbot.

The police submitted their report which outlined the details of the case and possible further avenues of investigation while Mrs. Emily Ann Talbot, mother of the deceased, gave evidence of identification. Those facts ascertained the coroner closed the inquest as there were a number of matters which needed further investigation by the police. The adjourned inquest would be held on Wednesday, March 5th at 2 o'clock. Immediately after Gaskin was taken before Mr. Mason where he was formally remanded until that inquest.

Reporters from the *Cannock Advertiser* at that first inquest stated that Gaskin "appeared to treat his position with the utmost unconcern and throughout the proceedings did not betray the least sign of distress".

At that second inquest Mrs. Talbot was first to give evidence. She stated that on Wednesday, February 19th at about 1.50 p.m. Thomas Saunders brought a note to her house for the deceased. Another daughter told her of the contents. Because of that note Elizabeth immediately dressed and left the house. She never saw her daughter alive again. On the Thursday morning at about 10.30 a.m. she had arrived at the prisoner's home in Bridgtown and questioned him as to what had happened on the Wednesday afternoon. He admitted to sending the note, but claimed that he did not see her. At that point she said that she was going to see the police and left.

In talking about her daughter's relationship with the accused Mrs. Talbot said that they had been married in July, 1913 and had lived with her. After he joined the army he had been on furlough for one week in February, 1918 when he lived with them and at that time there was no "unpleasantness". She also told the hearing that her daughter had two children, both of whom were not by Thomas Gaskin.

In reply to the coroner Mr. Tench, Gaskin's solicitor, said that he would not question the witnesses if they were going to appear at the magistrates' court later.

Thomas Saunders, a stoker at West Cannock Colliery, who lived at 83 Brindley Heath stated that on the Wednesday he saw the prisoner in the Anglesey Hotel, Hednesford about noon. After being asked if he lived at Tackeroo by the accused the witness delivered a note to the Talbots' home.

Thomas Henry Borton, chief sales clerk of the Cannock and Rugeley Colliery Company, stated that on Wednesday, February 19th at about 2.30

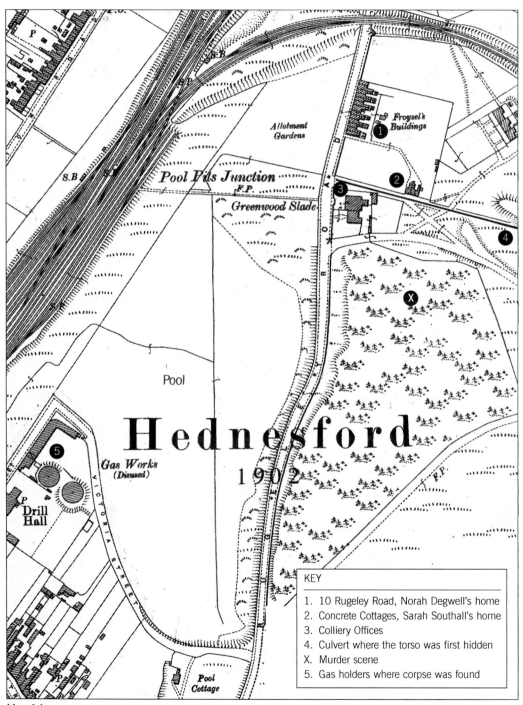

KEY

1. 10 Rugeley Road, Norah Degwell's home
2. Concrete Cottages, Sarah Southall's home
3. Colliery Offices
4. Culvert where the torso was first hidden
X. Murder scene
5. Gas holders where corpse was found

Map 14.

p.m. he saw, from the office window, a young man and woman walking along the Rugeley Road towards Hednesford. The woman was talking loudly which attracted his attention and they stopped near the fence by the plantation opposite the offices. The man got over the fence into the woods and the woman walked up the path towards the Valley Pit. She eventually went into the woods, but he saw neither of them again.

Questioned as to how they were dressed the witness said unfortunately he would not be able to recognise either again, but he had seen the prisoner when in custody. However, he could not swear that it was the same man, but he resembled the man he had seen.

Mrs. Sarah Southall, living at 31 Concrete Cottages, Rugeley Road said that she was looking through her front window which faced the path leading to the Valley Pit when she saw a woman wearing a long coat walking down that path along the side of the plantation and heading towards the pit. A man came out of the plantation in a crouching position and went towards her, although she did not see him join the woman as they became lost from view. She did not see the man's face, but he was wearing a dark suit. The woman was of slim build.

Footnote:- From a witness point of view the evidence of the last two was very sketchy as neither could actually identify either Elizabeth or Thomas Gaskin. Today's courts would probably not want to hear from them.

The most damning evidence was to come from the police. Superintendent Morrey stated that at about 4 p.m. on Friday February 21st he and Inspector Woolley met Gaskin as he was going to work at West Cannock Colliery and took him to Hednesford Police Station where they arrested him on the suspicion of causing his wife's death. On Sunday February 23rd the witness received a message which said that the prisoner wished to see him. Arriving at the police station Gaskin said that he would take them to the body. He also added, "She is in pieces. I cut her head off and tried to cut her leg off, but that is holding on by the sinews." Sergeant Heath was a witness to that statement.

After that a taxi was found and the witness, Sergeants Brough, Harrington and Heath accompanied Gaskin to Victoria Street,

Hednesford. When opposite the Gas Works Gaskin stopped the taxi and everyone got out. He then said, "Come here," and scaled a five foot wall into the compound. When we all reached the gas holder the prisoner said, "She is here," pointing to the tank containing the water. Once the dragging commenced Gaskin said, "I will take you and show you where I did it," and so I, Sergeant Wright, Constable Bates and the prisoner got back into the taxi and went to the plantation next to the Rugeley Road.

The prisoner then led us into the wood until we reached some fir trees where he stopped and said, "I did it here. This is where I cut her up." He had hidden her stockings, shoes and hat beneath some peat and stones. He then picked up a piece of stick and said, "This is what I stuck down her throat." Leaving that scene we arrived at the fence next to the road. Once more the prisoner stopped and said, "I dragged her here from there and cut her head off and nearly cut her leg off. This was when I came later the same night. I put her trunk in a culvert across there and took the head and clothes and put them in the gas holder. After I had been spoken to by two Hednesford policemen on Thursday night I came and dragged the body out of the culvert and took it to the gasometer. I pierced a piece of gas piping through the body and after that put it into the water."

*Not said in evidence in court, but noted by the police was that as he described the actual crime Gaskin became physically excited as though he were reliving the scene.

Superintendent Morrey continued his evidence saying that the prisoner said that he had taken a wheel barrow from the colliery on the Wednesday to wheel the corpse to the gas holder, but realised that it would leave an impression on the ground as it had snowed. Instead he left the barrow near the corner of the wood.

Finally Morrey stated that at 8 p.m. on the Sunday evening the prisoner made a written statement detailing all that he had told them that day. Apart from describing the actual crime it contained an account of the conversation Gaskin had with his wife before the crime. It read;-

Elizabeth:- *Why don't you come down home.*
There's nobody there, only mother and dad.

Gaskin:-   *Come in the wood and we'll talk things over.*

Details were then written of the conversation in the wood in which Gaskin accused his wife of infidelity, her attempts to get him to go home with her and his refusal to do so. It continued,

Elizabeth:- *Well. If you don't intend to do something to keep me, I shall go back to Monty. He promised to keep me if you wouldn't. But do come home with me.*

At that she started to cry and put her arms round my neck. I then put my left arm round her neck and gripped her throat.

Gaskin:-   *You dare to ask me to go with you after what you've done. You dare to tell me you'll go back to Harris.*

She struggled free and attempted to scream, but I grabbed her again.

Gaskin:-   *You are a she-devil of the first water and I'll send you to where you belong. You have had your pleasure while I was in France, now I'll tear your inside out.*

*It was then that Gaskin's account of the actual murder was read out to the hearing, but the newspapers refused to print the actual details of the crime as they were too gruesome. In fact it was said at the time that one juryman had to leave to be violently sick and another almost fainted when the details were disclosed.

Also in that statement were further details of what happened after the murder. He said that he had gone home, reaching there about 5.30 p.m. and had then gone to the cinema in Walsall Road, Cannock with his brother. About half an hour later he left and

49. Elizabeth Gaskin.

returned to Hednesford by bus and went to dispose of the body.

Sergeant Heath testified that he was present when Gaskin told Superintendent Morrey where the body could be found, adding that Gaskin himself helped to drag the water. When

the torso was found the skirt was wrapped around it. Later Mrs. Talbot identified it as her daughter's.

Inspector Woolley stated that when they arrested Gaskin at the pit they discovered a knife and a flash lamp. At 7 p.m. on the same day he and Sergeant Harrington went to 43 Longford Lane, Bridgtown where they took possession of a dark suit of clothes, a cap and shirt. In the suit pocket was note paper which had distinct markings. It later matched the paper on which a message had been received by Mrs. Talbot on Saturday, February 22nd. Dated February 20th and with the postmark of February 21st, 1919 at 12.05 p.m. it read:-

> *Lizzie is quite all right, she is with me now. I met her at Hednesford on Thursday. She was crying she told me her husband was making a fool of her, so I told her to leave all and come with me. She will send you some money when we get to London. We are going there next week. She will write herself when we get there, she is very upset now. I assure you she will be all right with me. Hoping you don't mind.*
>
> *From Lizzie's friend, W. Brooks.*

Continuing Inspector Woolley stated that when the clothes recovered from Gaskin's home were examined there appeared to be blood stains on the suit and cuff of the shirt.

The final witness was Dr. J. K. Butter who had carried out the post mortem. He gave graphic details of the many wounds that the deceased had suffered and testified that they were "consistent with the prisoner's statement to the police". He said that death was due to the extensive wounds, shock and loss of blood. However, in his estimation death was not due to strangulation, but to the many wounds. (Once again the newspapers decided it was best not to disclose the exact state of the deceased's corpse because of its mutilated condition.)

All the evidence heard the jury had no difficulty in declaring a verdict of "Wilful Murder" and Gaskin was remanded in custody until March 13th to await the magistrates' hearing. Immediately after the inquest he was taken by taxi to Winson Green Prison in

50. Postcard of the main scenes of the crime.

Birmingham. (Usually prisoners were sent to Stafford Gaol to await trial, but at that time Stafford Gaol had been closed and was awaiting a Government decision as to its future.)

On Thursday March 13th Gaskin was brought before the Magistrates Court at the Cannock Police Court. Hearing the case were Messrs. Bumsted, Mason and Gallatley while Mr. Pearce represented the Prosecution and Mr. Tench for the Defence. Mr. Pearce opened by saying that the case was "considerably lightened by statements made to the police by the prisoner, but would have to be further supplemented by witnesses".

Mrs. Emily Ann Talbot was first to give evidence and repeated her testimony given at the inquest. However, she was not to escape questioning at the magistrates' hearing. Mr. Tench asked about Elizabeth's condition at the time of the marriage to Gaskin suggesting that Elizabeth may have been suffering from a "specific disease" (quite probably syphilis or gonorrhoea). Mrs. Talbot hotly denied that inference. As to Gaskin being deceived about the pregnancy before the marriage Mrs. Talbot said that even she did not know that her daughter was pregnant before the marriage, but afterwards her daughter had told her that the child was not Gaskin's.

Continuing Mr. Tench suggested that Elizabeth had had two children while the prisoner was at Portland and before he joined the Army, but again Mrs. Talbot vehemently denied it stating that there were only two children born, one in Lichfield Workhouse and one at home. However, she had to admit that her daughter's Army Allowance had been stopped while her husband was serving and her character was being enquired into.

Under further questioning Mrs. Talbot admitted that her daughter had been "walking out" with a soldier from the Camp whom she believed lived at Cannock and that he was the father of her last child. Finally, she agreed that she knew that Gaskin had wanted a divorce and that her daughter had told him that Monty Harris would look after her if he would not.

The blackening of Elizabeth's character was an obvious ploy by the Defence to show mitigating circumstances in the murder.

Besides those witnesses who had come forward at the inquest there were others who could add further information in the case. John Thomas Garry, who lived at 22 Bradbury Lane, stated that he had been with Gaskin in several public houses, including the Uxbridge Arms and

Anglesey Hotel, on the morning of February 19th and they had several drinks together. They left the Plough and Harrow at about 2 o'clock, the witness going to Wimblebury and the prisoner going towards Hednesford. Gaskin said that he had an appointment, but did not disclosed what it was. However, he appeared "quite normal" at the time.

Sixteen year old Norah Degwell, who lived near the bridges on Rugeley Road (probably the Froysel Cottages) said that she was standing on her doorstep between 2.45 and 3.00 p.m. on February 19th when she saw Mrs. Gaskin and a man walking towards the Colliery Offices on the Rugeley Road. Mrs. Gaskin was talking loudly at the man who she later recognised as the prisoner. The deceased was wearing a white pinafore under her mackintosh.

Joseph Roadway, living at Bradbury Lane stated that he saw Gaskin near Lee's Farm, opposite the West Cannock Colliery Offices at 4.15 p.m. on the Wednesday. They spoke to each other and he remembered that the prisoner was wearing a dark grey suit and a plaid cap. He seemed quite sober.

Daisy Winfer of 47 Longford Road, Bridgtown said that she saw the prisoner in Church Street, Cannock on the Wednesday. It was almost 5 o'clock and they both got on the same bus to Bridgtown and spoke to one another. When they got off the bus she saw him go into his house.

When questioned by Mr. Tench Daisy said that she lived next door to the prisoner and in 1917, when he was on furlough, she overheard a quarrel between Gaskin and his wife. It was on a Sunday and she saw him fetch a gun out of the house and threaten to shoot his wife. She had to admit that on that occasion he had "a strange look in his eyes". She also said that he "was peculiar in his manner at times" and "seemed to be desirous of being alone since he was demobilised".

Cross examined by Mr. Pearce for the Prosecution Daisy said that he did not look "so peculiar on that day" (meaning the Wednesday) as she had seen him. However, she had seen little of him in recent years. She had seen him when he was on furlough in 1918, but only in passing since he had left the Army.

When Dr. Butter was examined Mr. Tench questioned him about Gaskin's behaviour in the past. The doctor said that he had known the prisoner all his life and he had been "very erratic in his ways". He had examined him when he went to school and he appeared quite normal then. He disagreed with the idea that he had "no will power". The last time he examined him he was quite all right and he did not think intoxicating drink would unduly upset him.

When questioned about a supposed incident in which Gaskin had tried to strangle himself with a scarf when he was a lad, the doctor was sure that he knew nothing of such an affair.

As to the articles removed from Gaskin's home and those found on him when he was arrested at the pit the doctor stated that there were marks of blood found on the trousers, pants and flannel shirt. There was also signs of blood on the knife. (At that time Blood Grouping was a relatively new science and the doctor had little knowledge of its procedure.)

Superintendent Morrey was also cross-examined by Mr. Tench. He said that he had known the prisoner for about eight or nine years and "though he had acted strangely at intervals he did not believe that Gaskin suffered from insanity at any period". When taken into custody he had been "quite rational in his actions". Finally Mr. Tench asked the superintendent if he believed everything that had been written in the prisoner's statement and Morrey replied that he did.

Because the case had taken so long (it was about 5.20 p.m.) the magistrates decided to continue the hearing the following morning. Only two more witnesses for the Prosecution were heard. James Bradbury of Mount Street, Hednesford said that he was the person who discovered the wheel barrow about twenty yards from the wood by the Valley Pit. Constable Heath produced the piece of gas piping which had been pushed through the deceased's body. He also stated that when taking the prisoner to Winson Green Gaskin said to him, "I have been under observation ever since I have been in prison. I thought of going potty, but I didn't want to be put in a straight jacket in a padded cell". He also told the hearing that Gaskin had said that he did not write the note to Mrs. Talbot, but that it was written at his dictation by a stranger whom he met outside New Street Station, Birmingham.

The final witness was Mrs. Williams, Gaskin's mother. She said that during her pregnancy with Thomas she had been ill for sixteen weeks and that might explain some of his behaviour. She said that he had been "strange in his manners all his life" and she had had him medically examined on several occasions. On one such occasion the doctor had said that he was "perfectly sane, but had no will power". Smoking caused him to tremble a good deal, but as she had only seen him the worse for drink on one occasion she could not say what effect intoxicants had upon him. She finished by saying that he had been a trouble to her all his life, even on one occasion attempting to strangle himself by pulling a scarf tightly around his neck.

Having listened to all the evidence the magistrates asked Gaskin how he pleaded. He declared "Not Guilty", but they had no hesitation in finding him guilty of "Wilful Murder" and committing him to trial at the Stafford Assizes.

On Friday July 11th Thomas Gaskin was tried for the wilful murder of his wife Elizabeth before Mr. Justice Roche. While the Prosecution concentrated on the horrors of the crime and the ways in which the prisoner made efforts to conceal his actions, the Defence relied on the poor behaviour of his wife and the possibility of Gaskin's insanity since an early age, exasperated by his wife's behaviour and his time at the Front. Mr. Milward for the Defence argued "Insanity moved in waves (in his client) and they might have a man shaky from youth, who might be so wrought upon by the blowing up of a mine in France and the drink partaken on the day of the deed, that when the moment came he was not right".

Knowing that the plea of insanity was his client's only real chance of escaping a possible death sentence Mr. Milward concentrated his efforts on proving that. Apart from producing the witnesses heard at the previous sessions he produced others. Ernest Woodhall, a miner from Chasetown, and Charles Dawson from Field Street, Blackfords testified that they had served in the same tunnelling company as Gaskin during the war and they were all buried in a counter mine explosion at the Front. That seemed to affect Gaskin's behaviour after and he used to leave the trenches to shoot at bottles and collect souvenirs under shell fire and frequently took unnecessary risks.

51. Funeral cortege March 2nd. 1919 performed by Stacey's Undertakers of West Hill.

Dr. Cassells, medical officer at Winson Green Prison, who had had the prisoner under observation and conversed with him during his time there, stated that he thought Gaskin was "of sound mind". However, under cross-examination he had to agree that the experience of the prisoner at the Front "might have affected his mental condition".

Such great play had also been made by the Defence on infidelity that the judge, in his summing up, felt obliged to warn the jury that under English law infidelity was not a crime and to look upon it as such was "nonsensical as well as a horrible suggestion". The jury took just half an hour to agree and found Gaskin guilty of "Wilful Murder". Before the judge passed sentence he asked Gaskin if he had anything to say. In a quiet and steady voice he simply said, "I did not intend to kill her." He was sentenced to death by hanging. That was carried out on August 8th, 1919 at Winson Green.

Footnote:- A petition of 6,000 signatures was sent to the Home Office for a reprieve, incredible as the area probably only had around 20,000 in total, that included children.

DYING FOR A RABBIT
Norton Canes 1893

Twenty nine year old William Masfen had two major passions in life - cricket which he played with Cannock Cricket Club and shooting. To further his hobby of shooting he had gained permission from Captain Harrison, a well-known local entrepreneur, to use his farmlands in Norton Canes for the sport. William's usual walk took him from his home at Rectory Cottage and around Hole Farm and the nearby fields. However, over the months he became suspicious that he was not the only one taking game in that area and so he determined to catch whoever was poaching the land. Frequently he was seen in the early hours out alone and unarmed searching the land for poachers.

He was soon proved right and on several occasions actually caught poachers red-handed.

In one incident it was rumoured that he confronted three or four men and took their poaching nets from them, having felled one who challenged him. Only days before the tragedy which was to happen he caught one Frederick Pearce who lived at Heath Hayes breaking branches off a cherry tree to get at the fruit. Pearce had pleaded with him not to tell the authorities and in return he would give William information about the poachers. That information concerned a family called Hewitt, a name well-known to William, who were supposedly going to be out poaching on the following Saturday.

On the evening of Friday, June 30th Masfen was out shooting with John Brooke, his father's gardener, and on their way back to Rectory

52. Rectory Cottage, Church Lane c.1920

53. Sketch of the crime scene.

Cottage William asked John to wake him at three o'clock the next morning as he was going to try and catch the Hewitts poaching. As requested Brooke woke him at three on the Saturday and William set off in the direction of Hole Farm. He refused help from Brooke saying he was more likely to catch them alone and, despite warnings, refused to take a gun or his dog.

Nothing was suspected for several hours, but by six o'clock Mrs. Masfen was worried about her husband and asked John Masfen, a cousin who was working at William Masfen Senior's farm on the Watling Street, if he would go and look for her husband. Failing to find any signs of William, John returned to Rectory Cottage and was persuaded to find the local constable to help in the search. Constable Treacy, John and Brooke set out again. While the constable and Brooke searched the outbuildings at Hole Farm John went towards a culvert, near to which a small brook ran. To his horror he discovered his cousin's body lying face-down in the stream with a wound in the left side of the head.

Once Constable Treacy had ascertained that William was dead he informed his superiors and soon Sergeant Upton of Cannock and Sergeant

Banton of Hednesford were at the scene. Strangely they removed the body from the culvert and had it taken to Rectory Cottage in a trap where Doctor Butter and Mr. Riley from Cannock examined it quickly, pronounced William dead and had the corpse removed to Cannock for a post mortem.

Meanwhile the police lost little time in tracking down the possible suspect, having been told by Brooke about the conversation on the previous night concerning the Hewitts. Having gone to the Hewitt's cottage in Stokes Lane several times during the day they eventually apprehended John Hewitt, a nineteen year old

54. Painting of Stoke's Lane cottages. The Hewitt family lived in the one on the far left.

55. Sketch of the Fleur de Lis. By 1900 the spelling had changed to Lys.

miner, and took him to Cannock Police Station.

John Hewitt denied all knowledge of the crime saying that he had been in bed until twenty minutes past five and when he got up his father and younger brother, Alfred, were already downstairs. He also claimed that he was still at home when his father, also John, had left for work at five thirty. As to the gun that was found at their house, John admitted using it on the Friday, but denied using it afterwards.

The inquest into the death of William Masfen began at 3.40 p.m. on Monday, July 3rd at the Fleur-de-lis Inn, Norton Canes in front of Mr. Jordan, the deputy coroner for the Stafford District. From the beginning he informed those present that it would be a short hearing just to lay before the jury the bare facts as then known as the police were still investigating the crime for further evidence.

The first witness was John Masfen who told the tragic story of how he was asked by Mrs. Masfen to search for the deceased and how he eventually made the terrible discovery of the corpse. (At that point in his evidence John burst into tears.) He then said that he had touched the body, but realising his cousin was dead he had called Constable Treacy who was about a hundred yards away. He arrived with Brooke and together they lifted the body from the stream. It

was at that point he noticed the head wounds. Unable to stay at the scene any longer he had left, but not before noticing that there seemed to be no signs of a struggle in the surrounding area.

He went on to tell the hearing that his cousin had often spoken of trouble with poachers on the farms and had even had some of them summoned at Cannock. Also when questioned by Josiah Trubshaw, the jury foreman, John stated that a man named Pearce had given information about poachers to escape punishment himself. They were to be around Hole Farm that Saturday and his cousin had planned to catch them.

Constable Treacy, stationed at Norton Canes, was next to give evidence. He stated that at about 8.15 a.m. on the Saturday John Masfen had arrived at his house and told him of the disappearance of the deceased. They immediately went in search of William Masfen and, together with John Brooke, they set off for Hole Farm. The witness and Brooke went towards the railway arch where he met a man named Cooper, the deceased's cowman, while John Masfen went to the culvert. As they searched the outbuildings at the farm John Masfen shouted that he had discovered a body. They then took the body out of the water and the witness noticed the head wound. He also saw blood and brains lying in the ditch.

Examining the clothing he discovered shot marks in the right side of the jacket and waistcoat. Searching the clothes he found £3 4s 6d and a halfpenny, along with a knife, a watch and chain, nine cartridges, several keys, a box of matches, paper and a pocket handkerchief. All those items led him to believe that robbery was not the motive for the crime. Also on examining the clothes further he found blood at the back of the shirt and a lot of shot marks at the back of the right shoulder. The remainder of the clothing was wet and muddy.

56. The barns on Hole Farm.

During his testimony one juryman asked the constable if he knew of any grievances between the deceased and the man arrested, but the coroner immediately intervened saying that the question could not be permitted at that hearing. (A point of law – hearsay evidence is not admissible and it was doubtful if Constable Treacy could have substantiated any possible incidents he might be able to relate.)

The final witness was Doctor Butter, the police surgeon who had completed the post mortem along with Mr. Riley on the Sunday afternoon. He stated that on the back of the head there was an irregular hole, four inches long and two inches wide, which had torn away the scalp, crushing and driving the bones of the skull into the brain tissue. The left ear was torn by several shots. On removing the scalp he had found that the bones were all fractured and the base of the skull was pulped, suggesting that the body had been severely struck around the head with a hard object.

There were indentures on the face which would be caused partly by blows and partly by shot. He had taken a large quantity of shot from the head, but there was nothing from the lower body. The back, shoulder and lower part of the right chest and lungs also contained lots of shot. In his estimation, and that of Mr. Riley, the deceased had been shot in the back and had then been beaten around the head with a solid object like a gun and then eventually, while still alive, had been shot in the head at close range.

When questioned by Mr. Ashmail, the lawyer for the Masfens and the husband of William's sister, Dr. Butter said that he did not think any blows were made by a fist. As to the actual death, he thought that the deceased "might have lingered after receiving the first shot, but the second was absolutely fatal".

It was at that point that the coroner adjourned the hearing to meet again on Friday, July 14th at 2.00 p.m.

Between those two hearings William Masfen was buried at St. James Church, Norton Canes on July 4th. The burial was organised by Joseph Sellman of Cannock and the chief mourners included William Masfen of Swan Farm, the deceased's father, Mrs. Ashmail and her husband, John Masfen and Mr. Hanbury Masfen of Tamworth, a cousin. Cannock Cricket Club were also represented by Mr. J. Roach. Unfortunately William's widow was too ill to attend.

57. Grave of William Masfen in St. James's Churchyard.

The adjourned hearing began with John Brooke testifying that on the Friday evening of June 30th he had been out shooting with the deceased and when they returned he left to go home to his cottage just opposite Rectory Cottage. However, after only a few minutes the deceased came to his croft and asked if the witness had heard any shots on Hole Farm that night. When he said that he had the deceased said that he would go out early the following morning to catch the poachers. When Brooke offered to accompany him Mr. Masfen said, "No, never mind. It's only those Hewitt chaps. I have had them before and I shall have them again." The deceased then asked to be woken at three o'clock the next morning and then left.

At 2.50 a.m. the witness got up and went over to Rectory Cottage and knocked the window with a line prop until he woke the deceased. Despite his warnings William went off in the direction of Hole Farm and he returned to bed. He did not see Mr. Masfen again until his corpse was found in the culvert.

The next witness was George Pearce, a miner living at Norton Canes (no relation to Frederick Pearce who had been caught and let off by the deceased). He told the hearing that he was well acquainted with John Hewitt and was with him from time to time in the afternoon and evening of Friday, June 30th until about 10.30 p.m. Three of them, himself, John Hewitt and a lad named Stackhouse, had gone for a walk along the canal side, over Sylvester Hedge, along a footpath and across some fields known locally as "the Roughs". They had turned up Wash Brook Lane, over Brook's Bridge and down to Stokes Lane to Hewitt's house. It was then about 5 o'clock.

At 6.60 p.m. he and Hewitt went out again with a gun towards the railway bridge in Stokes Lane. The gun belonged to Hewitt and it was the one produced in court. At about 9.15 p.m. Hewitt shot at a rabbit near Hole Farm, but missed and so they returned to the Hewitt's house. As it was about 10.30 p.m. he went home.

William Read, a farm labourer from Norton Canes, testified that on the morning of July 1st at 3.15 a.m. he was on his way to mow a field with his father and when they arrived at about 3.30 a.m. they heard a report from a gun. The sound came from the direction of the Hole Farm

buildings. Thinking nothing of it they began to work, but after ten or fifteen minutes they heard another shot which came from the same direction. Unfortunately as it was still very dim they saw little except for the outline of the tops of the buildings. However, he remembered his father saying that Mr. Masfen was "up early shooting".

Albert Osbourne, an assistant at Clark's Ironmongers in Cannock, stated that he knew John Hewitt, Senior, who used to visit the shop. They had started to repair a gun for him and on June 30th he had come into the shop to collect it. Unfortunately the repair was not finished, but John Hewitt, Senior had asked for a shillings worth of No. 6 cartridges. When he was informed they had none in stock he had twelve No. 5 instead. The cartridges then produced in court were identified by Osbourne as those sold to Hewitt. He said that he knew them as the cases had been slightly damaged and he had not sold any similar for some time. However, he had to admit that that was their only identification mark.

Unlike the first hearing it was Mr. Riley who appeared next. He stated that he agreed with the evidence given by Dr. Butter at the first inquest. Under questioning he confirmed that he too believed that the first shot did not kill the deceased, but the second surely did. As to the blow to the skull he said that he could not be certain if it came before or after the second shot.

If matters were looking grim for young John Hewitt it was the next witness who was to seal his fate. Sergeant William Upton of Cannock Police Station told the hearing that he had been called to the Masfen home at about 10.30 a.m. on Saturday July 1st. and saw the deceased's corpse. He then went to Hole Farm to examine the scene where Superintendent Barrett of Brownhills showed him some marks on the bottom rail of a fence. They had been caused by heavy nailed boots. The grass around the fence was trodden down by several feet and it looked like there had been a struggle. Searching further he discovered footmarks in the long grass and followed them into a nearby orchard and across a piece of meadow between the orchard and the railway. There he found recent marks leading up the railway embankment, which crossed the line and led down the other side, heading in the

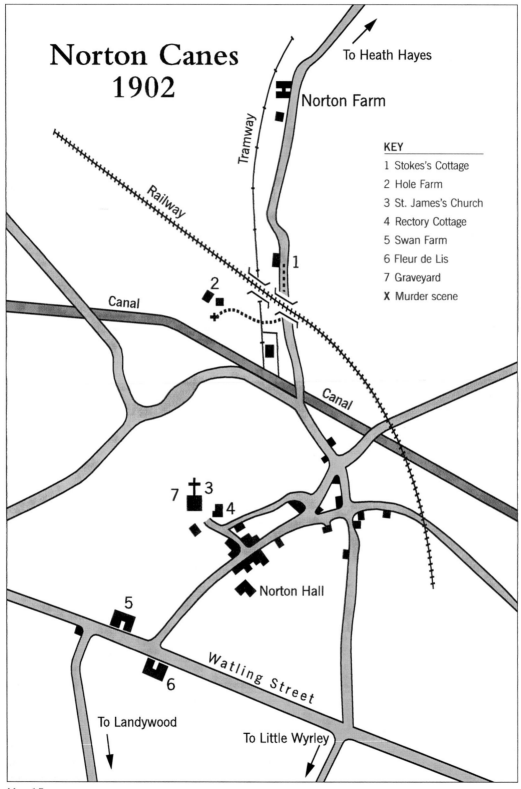

Norton Canes
1902

To Heath Hayes

Norton Farm

Tramway

Railway

Canal

KEY

1 Stokes's Cottage
2 Hole Farm
3 St. James's Church
4 Rectory Cottage
5 Swan Farm
6 Fleur de Lis
7 Graveyard
X Murder scene

Canal

Norton Hall

Watling Street

To Landywood

To Little Wyrley

Map 15

direction of the prisoner's house. At a point in Meanley's Meadow, almost opposite Stokes Lane cottages, he met with Mrs. Hewitt and they spoke of the deceased's death. At that time he turned back and retraced his steps.

However, later that day he and Superintendent Barrett went to the Hewitt's cottage in Stokes Lane, speaking first of all with John Hewitt, Senior. They discovered a gun at the house which had been recently fired and "roughly wiped" and were told that it belonged to John, Junior. They were then shown eight No. 5 cartridges, those produced in court. Still needing more evidence they asked to examine the boots of both father and son and proceeded to take them to the crime scene.

At a place near an occupation road leading to Hole Farm was a heel print with fourteen nail marks and it matched the heel of the prisoner's boot. Further along on the railway were other prints which had been covered over to protect them. They corresponded exactly in size to the prisoner's boots. They were larger than the father's prints, but showed no nail marks.

Back at the crime scene they discovered further evidence - three light coloured, waived hairs, apparently out of a person's moustache which matched young John Hewitt's hair. On returning to the cottage they also discovered a freshly skinned rabbit with some No. 5 shot in it. Both the prisoner and his mother were adamant that it had been killed the day before in Price's Field. At that point the officers left the house.

They returned again at about eight o'clock that night and asked young Hewitt to accompany them to Price's Field and show them where he had shot the rabbit. Once there he could not and worse, there were no signs of rabbits anywhere in the field. They then asked him to accompany them in a trap to Hole Farm and after further questioning they arrested him and took him to Cannock Police Station.

On arriving at the station the prisoner made his statement. He said that he had got up at 5.25 a.m. and started work at 5.45 a.m. His father and brother were already up and his father had left for work three minutes before he did. As to the gun he said that he had not used it since the Friday afternoon at about 2 o'clock.

Sergeant Upton then went on to tell the hearing that Hewitt had changed his story twice during his stay in the cells. At 3.25 a.m. on the morning of Monday July 3rd the witness went to the prisoner's cell to see that he was all right. The prisoner seemed to have been crying and when asked how he was he said to the sergeant, "I'm all right, but I would like to know how you think the job will go?" The witness told the hearing that he had replied, "It all depends on how it was done. I have known cases where men have been shot in poaching affrays while struggling with a gun." At that point the prisoner wanted to change his story and make a new statement.

The new statement made in front of the sergeant and Constable Jackson read,

"I, John Hewitt, went out at a quarter past two on the morning of July 1st, 1893. I took with me my gun and six cartridges No. 5 shot. I went from my father's house over the railway and through the orchard. I then went down to the place where Mr. Masfen's body was found. I was going to get over the rails when Mr. Masfen came out of the cart shed and wanted to take the gun from me. We were wrestling together when the gun accidentally went off, hitting him in the head. This was while I was trying to get over the rails. I had not been to bed that night, but had been asleep on the sofa all night. The rabbit was one I shot before meeting with Mr. Masfen. He wanted the rabbit and the gun. I told him he could have the rabbit but not the gun. He tried to get the gun off me when it accidentally went off."

Sergeant Upton then told the hearing that the prisoner had made yet another statement after the initial inquest. In it Hewitt stated,

"I struck Mr. Masfen on the head with the butt end of the gun after the first shot which hit him in the back of the head. I had both barrels loaded and the blow knocked the left hammer off the gun and broke the catch of the lever. The screw in the hammer had been out and lost for some weeks. Mr. Masfen fell over the rails into the ditch when I struck him on the head with the gun."

Sergeant then pointed to the statements produced in court upon which the prisoner had written, "I have read both statements which are correct, J. T. Hewitt."

Why exactly young Hewitt changed his story was not made clear, except that he might have thought that the court would be more lenient if they thought the shooting was accidental. Sergeant Upton had possibly led him to believe so which created something of a storm of protest later on. However, with the post mortem result telling a different story the jury were in little doubt as to their decision. John Hewitt was found guilty of "Wilful Murder" and sent to await trial at the next Stafford Assizes.

58. St. James's Church, Norton Canes c.1930.

In the meantime a rather strange event happened which might have given Hewitt a glimmer of hope. A man called William Cole from Heath Hayes gave himself up to Constable Dodge saying that he was responsible for the murder. He was taken to Bilston Station where he made a full confession. In it he stated that he had left his lodgings at about two o'clock on the morning of July 1st. and walked towards Norton Canes where he saw Mr. Masfen. A little further on he met John Hewitt carrying a gun. Hewitt pointed out Masfen and asked Cole to "have a go at him" with the gun. He replied that he had never shot a gun in his life, but had a try and hit the man. He only shot once.

Mr. Walters, his appointed lawyer, wired the details to Superintendent Barrett and on Saturday July 16th Sergeant Upton went over to Bilston to interview Cole. He immediately recognised Cole and became suspicious. Investigations proved beyond any doubt that Cole could not have possibly been near the murder scene on the fatal day as he was at work at the exact time of the shooting. In fact when he had sobered up he had already admitted that he had made up the whole story.

Subsequent investigations revealed that Cole was in the habit of admitting to crimes that he had not committed. About thirteen years previously, when in prison, he had confessed to the prison chaplain that he was the murderer of a man called John Ball of Longwood, near Aldridge. Investigations into that confession proved that he was in fact in Stafford Gaol doing fourteen days for other offences.

Despite his obvious innocence the police decided to teach him a lesson in the hope that he would never bother them again - they jailed him to await trial at Stafford Assizes along with Hewitt.

The trail began on Wednesday, July 26th, 1893 before Mr. Justice Collins and with no further witnesses to be introduced other than those at the two inquests it did not take long and the jury were in no doubt that John Hewitt had intentionally killed William Masfen. He was sentenced to be hanged in Stafford Gaol. As to Cole, he was quickly dealt with and warned as to his future behaviour by the judge. He was forced to sign the pledge that he would never drink again and was discharged.

Immediately after sentence Mr. Richard Mortiboy, one of the jurors, took it upon himself to organise a petition for clemency and letters were written to the Home Office to try to have the sentence reduced to life imprisonment. The main arguments of the memorial as it was known were:-

1. The condemned man was only nineteen years old and, despite his obvious guilt, there was no evidence to prove premeditation.

2. On the contrary, the evidence of Pearce proves that the prisoner did not know that Mr. Masfen was going to meet him.

3. The witness, Pearce, betrayed the prisoner just to save himself from court.

4. The prisoner, faced with such a powerful man as the deceased and fearing physical harm to himself, impulsively raised his gun to protect himself.

5. The constant change of confessions prove that the prisoner acted on impulse.

6. In meetings with his relatives in gaol since the verdict he has constantly maintained that he acted in self-defence.

Unfortunately the Home Office did not agree and on Saturday, August 12th the prison governor, Major Leggett, received a reply from Geoffrey Lushington of the Home Office informing him that there was not found "sufficient grounds to justify him in advising Her Majesty to interfere with the due course of the law".

During his stay in prison Hewitt wrote two letters, one to his favourite uncle and aunt and the other to his parents. In the first to his uncle and aunt, Clara, written before he knew of the failure of the plea for clemency, he begs their forgiveness, but defends his actions by saying:-

"..... hoping you are not put out because of my doing that dreadful deed, and hope you will forgive me for doing it. You know that it should have been too easy to have done it wilfully. I should not have done it if he had not started to take the gun off me. I asked him to let me be. I said, "You know my name and why not let me go?" He said, "I shall not let you go until you have given me the gun." But I refused to give it to him and I expect you would have done the same."

He continues:-

"Tell little Fred not to think about me doing that crime, but tell him not to follow my footsteps, because I know he has got a temper like his cousin Jack had got at that moment and he must not be angry with his parents."

Later in the letter he writes:-

"But I can't help it. I was in a passion when the deed was done. You know what a passion I had got when they did wrong to me. My passions were too strong for me. Mr. Masfen could not hold me at all, but still he would not give in."

The second letter to his parents is much more remorseful. Written on August 7th he does not mention the crime, but merely says farewell to his friends and family.

"O my dear parents I hope you will be as happy now as you were when I was at home and give my love to all of my friends and tell them there is no hope of seeing me any more in the old lane playing on that accordion of my father's. Tell little Fred to keep my pigeons in remembrance of me and tell him to be as happy as he can and give all my love to all the children. When they ask about me tell them I shall come back again. Don't forget to give my very best love to William Hollowood because I know that he is thinking of me all the day long and also to my uncle Tom and Mary Hewitt and give all my love to Alice Hill and tell her to try and get me off her mind for she thought much about me.

So goodbye my dear and kind-hearted and loving parents and do not think none the worse for me for I shall be better off than being in this world."

On Friday, August 11th Hewitt's father, mother, sister, Agnes, and his youngest brother, William, visited the prison to say their last farewells. His father told him that he thought there was little hope of a reprieve and hoped that his son would die "a Briton". Young Hewitt replied that he would and continued, "It was my life or his that morning and I struck him in self-defence, just as anyone else would have done."

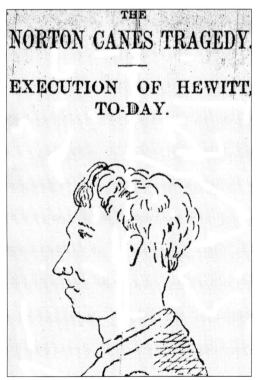

59. Sketch of John Hewitt drawn at his trial.

That was the last they would see of their son. On Tuesday morning, August 15th, soon after eight o'clock a crowd gathered outside Stafford Gaol to await the raising of the black flag, the signal of the actual execution. At twenty minutes to nine a group of four miners arrived, having walked all the way from Norton Canes (they had set out at a quarter past five that morning). They were there to pay their last respects to William Masfen, whom they regarded as "a merciful man who had let off scores of persons he had caught poaching on his land".

Meanwhile in the gaol Hewitt had eaten a hearty breakfast consisting of a pint of milk and sixteen ounces of bread, the usual fare for a condemned man. At a quarter to nine the procession, consisting of the chaplain, Reverend Goldney, the governor, the under sherriff, Mr. Everitt, the prisoner doctor, Dr. Scott, Mr. Chetwynd and Scott, the executioner, guided their charge towards the gallows.

A reporter from the *Midland Evening News* described Hewitt as "ghastly pale - white to the lips, but his small grey eyes were full of keenness. There was no stupor, no prostration - the man was perfectly collected" as he stepped towards the ropes.

By nine o'clock the execution had taken place and the inquest into the cause of the prisoner's death and its execution (a formality to make sure everything had been carried out correctly) had begun immediately after death. Not long after that a burial service took place in the little cemetery at the back of the prison chapel and as the reporters and inquest jury departed they could see lime being poured on to the coffin.

60. Memorial plaque to the Masfen family in St. James's Church.

Footnote:-

1.Strangely Frederick Pearce went to Stafford to witness the execution and was chased by an angry crowd around the town until he took refuge in a local inn until the crowd had dispersed.

2. Local rumours had it that the police got the wrong man. People in Norton Canes were convinced that John Hewitt, Senior, was the man confronted by William Masfen and he persuaded his son to take the blame thinking that the authorities would not execute such a young person. Those rumours persist today and when I chatted with a distant relation of young John Hewitt he was strangely not alarmed by those rumours. It is not for your author to make any judgements, but I just hope the police were correct.

A LUCKY ESCAPE
Pye Green 1900

Farmers and landowners in the past (and even today in some cases) always had the problem of poaching and when winter came around and food was at a premium for the needy the problem usually became worse. The trouble was that it meant that those involved in the nefarious activity often carried weapons and that meant that there was danger for anyone who might try to stop them. Hunger might have made them desperate men, but in many cases the game caught was purely a way of supplementing their own income and they were not about to let any landowner stop them earning that extra cash. It was just such a situation into which Samson Blewitt stumbled on Friday February 9th, 1900.

Between five and six o'clock on that evening he left his farmhouse at Pye Green to attend a number of his cattle and while doing that work he noticed two men acting suspiciously in a field near to the farm. They were obviously trying to keep out of sight and so he presumed that they were in search of game around the farm. Rather than involve the police who would take some time to reach his farm he went towards them himself. As he neared the men he noticed that one of them was carrying a gun, but undeterred he moved closer and ordered them off the land.

Rather than make a run for it, the taller man raised the gun to warn Blewitt off, but the farmer was having none of that and moved to within thirty yards. Suddenly the taller man pointed the weapon at Mr. Blewitt and fired peppering him with shot. He took shots in both thighs, in his hand, some on the shoulder and left arm and most serious of all were the shots to his neck. His assailants then ran off, but in spite of his injuries Mr. Blewitt followed them until they reached the boundary of his farm. There the men turned and again pointed the gun, that time

61. Samson Blewitt.

threatening to kill their pursuer if he continued to follow them.

Realising they probably meant business he did not move any nearer and the poachers made off. He then turned to seek assistance and, meeting two miners, asked them to help him follow the poachers. When they refused he simply continued to follow in the direction of the poachers and once again saw them, but they had then separated. As it was futile to try to track either man he returned to the farm and then drove to Hednesford Police Station where he reported the incident to Sergeant Whitehurst.

Sergeant Whitehurst and Inspector Burgess, assisted by P.C. Johnson, having got a description of the two poachers, immediately began their investigations. By the Sunday they had arrested Thomas Jenkinson of Mount Street, Hednesford and by the Monday they had detained George Jenkinson, late of Burgoyne Street, Hightown and then living at Nuneaton where he had worked for some time.

On the afternoon of Tuesday February 13th the two men appeared before Mr. F. Bumstead at Cannock Police Court. They were charged with intent to do grievous bodily harm to Samson Blewitt. Depending on the outcome of the hearing they could be charged with attempted murder.

P.C. Johnson of Chadsmoor stated that on the evening of Friday February 9th he went with Sergeant Whitehurst to the house of the prisoners' father in Burgoyne Street and George Jenkinson was there. He informed George that he had come to make inquiries about the shooting of a man at Pye Green and that he had been told that George was one of two men seen in the area at the time. George Jenkinson replied, "I have never had a gun since I went to Nuneaton. I have not been out of the house since three o'clock when I came in and lay on the sofa."

On the Saturday the witness tried to find George Jenkinson again, but failed to find him. On the Sunday he visited the house of Thomas Jenkinson in Mount Street and failed to find him also. However, by the Monday George Jenkinson was delivered to the local police station by the Nuneaton Police along with two guns recovered from the house where he lived. On being charged George Jenkinson replied, "I know nothing about it. I have no guns except those that came from my house (meaning Nuneaton)." It was then that Inspector Burgess read a statement to the prisoner which his brother, Thomas, had made. Immediately George said, "You can't prove now how the gun went off."

Sergeant Whitehurst then gave evidence. He stated that on Sunday evening he, along with the constable and Inspector Burgess, visited the home of Thomas Jenkinson, Senior, again and that time Thomas, Junior, was there in bed. When he came down into the kitchen he immediately said, "I know nothing about that shooting case, so you needn't come to me about it." The father then tried to help his son by saying that Thomas had been in the house since three o'clock and had not left it. Unfortunately, as the witness

pointed out to Thomas, no one had mentioned a shooting and if he had been in the house since three o'clock how did he know about it. The old saying "give someone enough rope and they will hang themselves" certainly applied there and so the police arrested Thomas.

Once at Hednesford Police Station he was charged, but was still adamant that he was not involved adding, "If you can bring anybody to prove that I was there I will plead guilty." On the evening he was moved to Cannock Police Station and by the Monday he had changed his story and made a statement which implicated his brother, George.

The sergeant then went on to tell the hearing that at 7 o'clock on the Monday evening he and Inspector Burgess went to a shed near a chapel in Mount Street (the Congregational Church) and found a gun. It was in two pieces and the left barrel had been fired. The right one was loaded but not capped.

Finally the sergeant read out Thomas's statement to the court. It read:- "I will tell you

62. Samson Blewitt with a friend, a local J.P. Taken c.1930. Who is the J.P.?

the truth about this. My brother asked me to go with him to Pye Green. Blewitt came to us, and he (George) shot at him. I was fairly taken to. You will find the gun in the shed near the chapel where I live. George told me to hide it. I am sorry. I have been waiting for you to come, as I wanted to tell you the truth about it."

At that point in the proceedings Mr. Aston, who was defending Thomas, asked that his client be discharged on account that there was no evidence against him trying to harm the farmer. However, Mr. Bumstead insisted that he face charges as well as his brother, but gave him bail on the two sureties of £10.

★Bail simply means that the person is not kept in prison until the trial, but should the prisoner not turn up for the court hearing then the money paid in surety is forfeited to the court. It is unusual to give bail in a shooting case.

George Jenkinson was remanded in custody until the trial.

At a special Sessions held at the Public Rooms, Cannock on Friday February 23rd before Mr. Bumstead and Mr. Wolverson George Jenkinson was charged with shooting Samuel Blewiit with intent to do him grievous bodily harm and Thomas Jenkinson was charged with being an accessory after the act.

Mr. George Barrett, a surveyor from Lichfield, produced a map of the incident detailing the various places on the farm where the incident took place and exactly where each person had been. However, the Defence objected to the map as it made certain references to guilt which, of course, had yet to be proved. A technical objection, but the court declared that the references on the map be "struck out".

Next to give evidence was Samuel Blewitt who stated that at about 5.20 p.m. on February 9th he was in a field known as Sixty Acre near his house carrying water for his cattle when he saw the two prisoners evidently trespassing in search of game. One of them was in the turnip field with a gun and the other was standing in the road near the hedge of the same field. The witness went towards them and the one in the field walked to the other and spoke to him. Afterwards he turned back and went down the side of the fence of the turnip field and got over the fence into the Sixty Acre Field. When the

63. Samson Blewitt with his trusted farmhand c.1930

witness got into the same field the man with the gun ran off and the witness followed.

Suddenly the man turned round, put the gun to his shoulder, pulled the trigger, but it misfired. The prisoner then ran off again and the witness pursued him. Again the man turned and threatened to shoot the witness if he came any nearer, but he advanced towards the prisoner who then shot at him. The witness was struck with a number of pellets. He stopped for a second or two and the man ran off. He then continued to follow until the farm boundary fence was reached. There the man got over the fence into Mr. Lee's land, known as Lee's Common. He was then joined by the other prisoner.

Once again the prisoner put the gun to his shoulder and the other prisoner told him to shoot if the witness came any nearer. Perhaps to save himself the witness said to the men, "You need not trouble, I am not after you," to which the prisoner holding the gun replied, "What the ——- are you running after then?" The witness

64. Haymaking on the farm. Believed to be the first bailing machine in the district. Samson's son, Edgar, is standing next to him.

then turned as if to go back home and the men went on a short distance. However, the witness was determined to follow and that time the prisoner said that he "would give him the full barrel if he stirred another inch". He once again turned back and the men went towards the tram road bridge.

When he saw that they had reached the bridge he turned again to follow, crossed the tram road and met a man coming from West Cannock Colliery. He asked the miner if he would go with him to see who the two men were who were on the bridge, but he refused. The witness passed under the bridge, where the two men stood, to go to his father's house. At that time he was relatively safe as there were two miners with him, one named Peake and the other Plant. When he got to his father's house he asked him to accompany him to Hednesford Police Station.

On Tuesday February 13th at about 11.00 a.m. he visited Cannock Police Station where he formally identified both Jenkinsons as the men whom he had seen on his land. The taller of the two, George, he identified as the one who shot him. Finally he told the hearing that on February 17th he had helped Mr. Barrett draw up the map

of the fields and then used it to explain to the court how the incident happened. When asked by Inspector Burgess, who acted for the Prosecution, how he had identified the men so quickly he said that he had known them from the past as he had forgiven them "times without number" for trespassing on his land.

When asked by Mr. Elliott for the Defence how he could be sure it was the prisoners on his land so late in the afternoon (remember it was early February) he said that it was beginning to get dusk, but there was sufficient light for him to identify the men who were three or four hundred yards away. As to George Jenkinson trying to kill him Samuel was adamant that the prisoner had deliberately shot at him and had threatened to shoot him dead if he went nearer. Also he insisted that Thomas had said, "Shoot him if he comes any nearer." As if to clarify his statement he showed the court how the gun had been held during the threats.

When questioned as to why he had not told the police who the men were at the first interview (Mr. Elliott was inferring that Blewitt had made up the names of known trespassers) Samuel insisted that he was upset at the time.

116

The next witness was to prove just how lucky Samuel Blewitt had been to survive the attack. Doctor Phillips of Hednesford said that he had examined Samuel on the evening of February 9th and discovered three small shot wounds in the front of the right thigh, four in the front of the left thigh, two on the outside of the left knee, one on the front of the left arm and one on the front of the right arm below the elbow, one on the back of the right hand and one on the right forefinger. However, most serious were two on the left side of the neck. The wounds punctured the skin, but fortunately none had damaged any vital organs and were unlikely to be dangerous. Because of that he had advised Mr. Blewitt to go home where he continued to attend him.

When questioned the doctor said that the position of the wounds made it clear that Mr. Blewitt was facing his attacker when the gun was fired.

The next witnesses were called either to prove that the Jenkinsons were in the vicinity of Pye Green on February 9th or that George sometimes carried a gun. Joseph Dodd, a labourer who lived at Hospital Cottage, West Chadsmoor, said that he had met the two men about three hundred yards from Blewitt's Farm as he was going from work. He spoke with them for about a minute or two and when he left them they headed towards Pye Green. Z. Jellyman of John Street, Chadsmoor, stated that on February 5th he was outside the Jolly Collier when he met George Jenkinson. The prisoner had the barrels of a gun inside his coat and the stock outside.

The final witnesses for the Prosecution were the police officers who told how they came to arrest both Jenkinson brothers with the inspector finishing by reading out Thomas Jenkinson's written statement.

Under cross-examination by Mr. Elliott there was some debate as to whether the prisoner had stated "shot at him" in his statement or "shot him". Inspector Burgess insisted Thomas had said "shot at him". The difference may seem to be really very trivial, but "shot at him" implies there was deliberate intent to hit, whereas "shot him" could imply an accident - the Jenkinsons' defence. Also Mr. Elliott questioned the police interpretation of George Jenkinson's supposed flight to Nuneaton, thus proving guilt. He maintained that his client "simply went to his home because that was where his wife and children were living".

In his summing up Mr. Elliott said that there was no real evidence against Thomas and asked the magistrate to dismiss the case against him. However, he stated that having heard the evidence against George he expected them to send him for trial (a case of double bluff?) and would waste their time no further save to say that the tale told by Mr. Blewitt was "a most incredible one" and the prisoners "absolutely denied the statements made by him". They were insistent that "the discharge of the gun was a pure accident".

The magistrates refused to dismiss the charge against Thomas and both prisoners were committed to trial at the next Assizes. However, once again Thomas was granted bail.

Justice was swift in Victorian times. There was no long wait for prisoners as there seems to be today. On Thursday March 8th the brothers were tried before Mr. Walton Q.C. and found guilty. For his minor role in the shooting Thomas was given one month in gaol while George received fifteen months hard labour.

BEARING IT ALL SECRETLY
Rawnsley 1915

Only since the advance of studies in human psychology have doctors realised that the mind is capable of dreadful decisions when under extreme stress. Despair and depression can frequently be followed by disaster if there is no one to help the sufferer overcome the situation. But what happens if those closest are themselves unable to ease the problem or, perhaps worse, what if they may have inadvertently helped to create the situation? Just such a problem would face twenty year old Lucy Olive Riley in January, 1915.

The tragedy began in the early months of 1913 when Lucy found herself pregnant, a dreadful plight for a young girl in those days. Think of all the shame it would bring to her parents in the small mining village of Rawnsley. The only person she could turn to was her mother, Hannah, who, worried as to how her husband might react, decided that the best place for Lucy was the Cannock Workhouse until she had had the child. The baby was to be their secret - what later would prove to be a fatal mistake.

On June 27th, 1913 Lucy entered the workhouse and Alfred George Spire, the Master, promised that all would be kept secret and eventually the child would be adopted. Just what Mrs. Riley told her husband, George William, about their daughter's "lodgings" can only be surmised, but he did not seem to want to see his daughter or ask any awkward questions. It was never made clear if he even knew of the whereabouts of his daughter.

Eventually the baby girl was born on September 25th and named Gwendoline May Riley. By early 1914 Mr. Spire had found someone whom he thought was suitable to foster the child, a Mrs. Jones of St. John's Road, Cannock. After a brief interview with Mrs. Riley it was decided that the child should be given over to Mrs. Jones who eventually decided to adopt her. Lucy was then removed from the workhouse in the March, but instead of going back home Mrs. Riley thought it best that her daughter live with an aunt at Leacroft (again Mr. Riley did not ask for any explanation). By the August Lucy had found a position in service in Hednesford in a respectable household, but her past was kept secret in case she was dismissed. Everything seemed to have worked out well, but fate has a way of interfering with happiness.

War had been declared in September, 1914 and it was not long before Enoch Jones was called up into the Reservists. Like so many "war widows" Mrs. Jones began to find it difficult to manage financially without her husband's wage and so in the January of 1915 she contacted Lucy to ask her to take back the little girl or at least help to pay for the child's upkeep. When Lucy seemed reluctant to have the baby Mrs. Jones went to Hednesford and, meeting Lucy near the station, forced her to take the little girl back.

Desperate Lucy turned to her sister, Annie Waltho, who offered to take the child in for the night, but no longer as she already had a child in arms at the time. The next evening Lucy returned and took the baby away and that was the last that the family saw of it alive. On the morning of Friday, February 13th the dead child was discovered floating in the Birmingham Canal at Hawkes Green.

By midnight on the same evening the police had arrested Lucy and taken her to the police station. Once there she was charged and made the following brief statement, "Mrs. Jones handed me the child. I took her home and my parents would not have her. My sister had her one night and would not have her any longer so I threw the child in the canal. I am sorry I did it."

65. Hednesford Canal Basin c.1930.

Despite having a confession from the young woman the law was bound to hold an inquest for two possible reasons. Firstly, all sudden deaths have to have an inquest despite the explanation being obvious in case the post mortem reveals unknown facts; and secondly, there might just be the possibility that the arrested person is not telling the truth and trying to protect the real criminal.

That initial inquest began on Tuesday February 16th at the Council Offices, Cannock before Mr. S.W. Morgan. He began by telling the jury that Lucy, as was her right in law, had declined to be at the inquest and so her statement made to the police at the time of her arrest was read out first. Harry Flavell, a boatman living at the back of 10 Park Road, Darlaston near Wednesbury, was first to take the stand. He said that he was working on the Birmingham Canal at Hawkes Green on the morning of February 13th. The boats were all jammed together and he was trying to move them out of the way to clear the waterway when he spotted something floating in the canal. He pulled the bundle out with his hands and discovered that it was a dead child. As he pulled the child out its

66. Constable Bates who mainly policed the Wimblebury and Rawnsley area.

dummy fell from its mouth. Obviously shocked he called to a man who was walking along the canal side.

Alfred Brindley, a farmer from Hawkes Green, was that man and he told the court that it was about 7.30 a.m. when the boatman called him over. They both examined the child carefully and, realising that it was dead, they sent a boy to inform Constable Bates. By 10.30 a.m. the constable and Inspector Morrey had removed the body.

Hannah Riley from 509 Littleworth Road, Rawnsley took the stand and related the story of her daughter's pregnancy, her spell in the workhouse and the adoption of the baby girl. She also said that once all seemed fine her daughter had managed to find a position with Mr. & Mrs. Stacey at West Hill in Hednesford and had been there some four months. (Ironically Mr. Stacey was Hednesford's undertaker, though it was not reported exactly who carried out the burial of little Gwendoline.)

Lucy had visited her about once a fortnight while she worked at West Hill and seemed happy. However, on January 18th when the witness went to her other daughter's house she was worried to find the baby girl there, but not Lucy. Having been told of the dreadful situation of Mrs. Jones handing back the child she was so worried that she planned to be back at her daughter's when Lucy arrived the next day to take the child away. On Tuesday January 19th her daughter arrived and pleaded with her sister to keep the baby, but she would not and so at 7.30 p.m. she left saying that she would return the child to Mrs. Jones.

Questioned by the jury Hannah said that she pleaded with her daughter to take the child back to Mrs. Jones and thought she was going to when she left. When she saw Lucy again on Thursday January 28th for a few minutes she looked worried and so Hannah had asked her about the child. Her daughter had simply said, "Oh, it's all right, mother, don't worry," and had then left the house.

Under closer scrutiny Hannah had to admit that they had deliberately kept the pregnancy and birth a secret from her husband for fear of what he might do. That was why she could not offer to take the child back to her home, although Lucy had never asked her to do so. Also it was her suggestion that her daughter go into the workhouse and have the child adopted when it was born. She had known of the adoption and had even interviewed Mrs. Jones before the adoption. They had drawn up an agreement which signed the child over to Mrs. Jones. It read, "This is to certify that Lucy Olive Riley gives the baby, Gwendoline May Riley, to Mrs. Jones. February 28th, 1914."

*Whether or not that document was registered is not known. Would it stand up in court of law if Lucy wanted the child back at a later date? Adoption in Victorian England between the poorer classes and those slightly better off or childless was not unusual, the natural parents often being paid for the child, though no payment was made in this case.

Alice Jones of 21 St. John's Road, Cannock told the hearing that sometime during the middle of February, 1914 she had an interview with Hannah Riley concerning the baby girl and then went to Cannock Workhouse and received Gwendoline May from Lucy Riley and then adopted her. She kept the baby until January 18th, 1915 during which time the mother came to see the child several times, but she never paid anything for the maintenance. Early in the January she wrote a letter to the accused and asked her to call on her. The accused replied that she could not do so at present, but would write back again.

On January 18th, accompanied by Mrs. Ellen Wright, a neighbour, the witness went to Hednesford with the baby first calling at Mr. Stacey's home. Finding the accused not at her place of work she proceeded towards

67. Station Bridge, Hednesford c.1910.

Hednesford and met her near Hednesford Railway Station with a young man. The witness said to Lucy, "I have come to see you about Gwendoline," and the accused replied, "I do not know what I can do. I am only getting 4 shillings a week." Mrs. Jones then said, "Well, I cannot keep her as my husband is at the Front and I am short of money." The accused then said, "All right," and continued, "I hope you have not told my employer. If you have they will turn me out."

Mrs. Jones then said that she handed the child to Lucy who seemed upset and began to cry. However, the witness then walked away and went home. On February 15th she read that a child had been found drowned in the canal at Hawkes Green and thought by the description of the clothing that it could be Gwendoline. She then contacted Superintendent Brookes who took her to the mortuary where she identified the child.

In reply to the foreman of the jury Mrs. Jones said that she had intended to keep the child and would have done so had it not been for her husband leaving for the Front and she having little money. When she adopted the baby girl she had every intention of keeping her for good. (Although their men were fighting for their country their wives found it very difficult to cope as money paid to their husbands for being in the Army was frequently delayed. In our area the miners paid into a fund to help those families who were struggling and food was often provided by pub landlords and local businessmen, but that did not suffice for losing the family income. (See *A History of Hednesford and Surrounding Villages* also by the same author.) She finished by saying that she had written to her husband telling him that she would have to take the baby back to the mother.

The coroner asked Mrs. Jones if she had made any suggestion to Lucy about possibly still keeping the child when she met her in Hednesford and Mrs. Jones said that she had, but the accused replied that she could not do much as she only earned 4 shillings a week. She added that her husband had another child to keep, which was not living with her, but she still had to pay for it.

Superintendent Grove then asked Mrs. Jones if she would have given the baby back if the accused had asked for her to which she replied that she would not. That brought about a sarcastic remark from the policeman who said, "When you got tired of it, you were quite willing to give it back to her." Annoyed Alice Jones replied, "I was not tired of it!"

At that point Mrs. Jones was told to stand down and Annie Elizabeth Waltho took the stand. She said that she was the wife of Bernard Waltho and lived at 431 Littleworth Road, Rawnsley. On the evening of January 18th her sister, Lucy, arrived at her house between 7 and 8 o'clock with a child in her arms. She asked if Annie would take the baby in for the night providing she fetched it back the next day. She and her husband agreed and Lucy left. The next day she wrote a note to her sister, sending it by messenger, and asked her sister to have the baby back. She signed her mother's name on the note as requested by her mother.

Her sister arrived between 7 and 8 o'clock and stayed for about an hour. During that time the witness pleaded with her to return the child to Mrs. Jones. She eventually left saying that she would go back to Mrs. Jones. Since that day she had seen her sister, but had not mentioned the child, neither had she asked what her sister had done with the baby.

When asked why she had not kept the child herself as the accused was obviously upset Annie said that she could not as she already had a baby in arms herself and her sister did not seem upset at the time. The coroner continued, "Was there a bit of a scene when you said you could not have it?" to which Annie replied, "No, she did not seem upset, although she cried." The coroner retorted, "Well, people don't cry as a rule unless they are upset, do they?" Annie did not reply.

When the coroner asked, "Weren't you curious to know what had become of the child?" Annie simply replied, "No." Changing tack the coroner then asked about the relationship of the accused and her mother and father. Annie said that her mother had always been kind to her sister about the child, but her father knew nothing of the affair. When asked why the child had been kept secret from their father Annie replied, "I think she was frightened of what father would say or do." With that Annie was stood down.

68. Dr. Butter with his chauffeur, Walter Bird.

Dr. Butter said that he had carried out the post mortem on the child and she was "a well developed and well nourished child weighing 17 to 18 pounds". The child must have been well cared for as the clothing was more than adequate for the time of year. It consisted of a bonnet, a woollen shirt, a pair of baby stays, a woollen bodice, flannel petticoat, linen skirt, blue cashmere frock, pinafore, jacket, socks and boots. As for the body, there were no signs of fracture to the limbs, but it was swollen and discoloured, "bleached, sodden and wrinkled" due to the time it had been in the water. In his opinion the body had been in the water one to two weeks or perhaps slightly longer. The cause of death was asphyxia by drowning.

The final witness was Inspector Morrey who had helped remove the body from the canal. He said that at about midnight on Saturday February 13th he, together with Sergeants Ledward and Brooks, went to Mr. Stacey's home and interviewed the accused. During the interview she became faint and it was some time before they could remove her to the police station and charge her with the offence.

Asked about the location of the body and the Waltho house the inspector said that it was about

69. Last remaining cottage on East Cannock Road c.1950.

one and a half miles from the house and one would have to pass the canal within about 200 yards on the way to Cannock where Mrs. Jones lived. There was a footpath at East Cannock which led from the road to the canal near to where the body was found. (The relevance of the

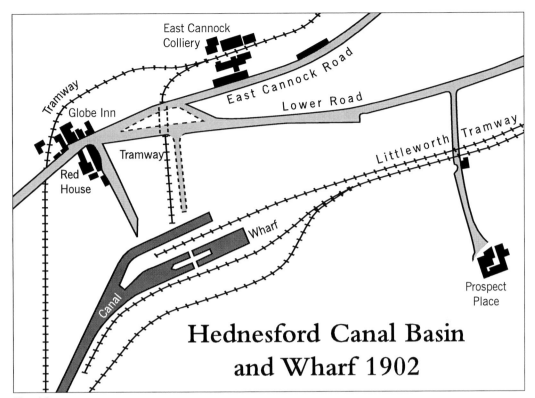

East Cannock
Colliery

East Cannock Road

Lower Road

Tramway

Globe Inn

Tramway

Littleworth Tramway

Red
House

Tramway

Wharf

Canal

Prospect
Place

Hednesford Canal Basin
and Wharf 1902

Map 16.

distances could be proof that Lucy had plenty of time to work out what she was going to do.)

In summing up the coroner said that the jury would have very little difficulty in reaching their verdict. He was afraid that there was only one verdict - wilful murder - but he thought it wise to consider the situation the accused found herself in on the fatal day. However, in reaching their verdict he stated clearly that "the crime had nothing to do with the jury. They were not concerned with the state of the girl's mind; their plain duty was to ascertain the cause of death". (A movement away from the Victorian idea of an inquest and closer to today's interpretation of the responsibility of an inquest.)

The jury, however, were obviously interested in the terrible situation that Lucy found herself in and Mr. Breeze asked about the father of the child and if he was paying towards its upkeep and whether Lucy's parents had done their duty to the girl. The coroner replied, "I am afraid that has nothing to do with the cause of death," to which Mr. Breeze retorted, "That was the cause of death, I think."

Obviously perturbed by the case Mr. Cole, another jury member, said, "I think Mrs. Jones is very much to blame. When she found she was not in a position to keep the child she ought to have taken it back to the Union Workhouse." Yet another juror said, "Everybody seems to have turned their back on the girl." The foreman then stated, "In face of all the circumstances related this afternoon I am in favour of making a very strong recommendation to mercy, if we are in order." The coroner replied, "When she comes up for trial at the Assizes, you mean. You can do that."

Still not finished another juror added, "I think she was treated very badly by her parents." Yet another, "She seems to have been chastised by everyone," and a final juror added, "Some of the witnesses have told untruths."

Clearly the jury were angered and emotionally disturbed by the case, but they were finally persuaded to give their verdict. They had no option but to return a verdict of "Wilful Murder", but with a strong recommendation to mercy.

On Tuesday February 23rd Lucy Olive Riley

was transferred from Stafford Gaol to the Public Rooms at Cannock for the magistrates' hearing before Mr. Bumstead and Mr. Gallatley. The wife of a policeman had to help her into the "Lower Deep" as the second court was called and Lucy looked worried and anxious and just as if she were about to collapse. Now and again the lady custodian offered her smelling salts and a police officer gave her a glass of water. She followed the proceedings very listlessly and when it came time for her to make her statement she almost collapsed, but somehow struggled through it.

70. Cannock Police Court c.1910. The photographer was A.D. Orton (1865-1927) whose descendants gave the picture to Cannock Chase Museum.

All the witnesses from the inquest repeated their evidence without any new facts appearing and the only other witness to appear was Alfred George Spire, Master of the Cannock Union Workhouse. He stated that the accused had been admitted to the workhouse in June 1913 in an advanced state of pregnancy. The baby girl was born on September 25th and given the name of Gwendoline May Riley. The child was removed from the workhouse on February 28th, 1914 by Mrs. Alice Jones and on March 5th Lucy left.

With the proceedings completed the magistrates gave their verdict – Lucy Olive Riley was charged with "Wilful Murder" and remanded to await trial at the Assizes. When asked if she had anything to say Lucy burst into floods of tears and said, "I don't remember doing it. I was so depressed and worried with all the troubles I have had. I had no one to help me through it. I have had to keep it to myself and bear it all secretly."

★As the court was rising a man came forward and said that he desired to secure the services of a barrister for Lucy. He said that the girl needed a friend and he would like to help her. He was not acquainted with the accused in any way, but had read of the case in the newspaper and simply wanted to help her. The court intimated that no doubt the accused would be defended and he better see a solicitor if he wanted to help. Spoken to after the hearing by a reporter he said that he was a comparative stranger to the district, but was greatly interested in the case.

No doubt the reporter thought that the man was possibly the father of the child and a good story or scoop was about to fall into his lap. However, like so many others in the area, he was just someone who had the deepest sympathy with Lucy Olive Riley.

The trial at the Assizes was on July 6th, 1915 before Mr. Justice Bray. Once again the same witnesses gave their evidence with Mrs. Jones and Hannah Riley coming in for some tough questioning. Mr. Bosanquet for the Defence asked Mrs. Jones if any payment for maintenance had been agreed upon when the adoption took place to which Mrs. Jones replied that there was to be none by the prisoner. She had adopted the child as she had none of her own and fully intended to look after it herself. When asked, "How did you think the accused was going to see to the child when you gave it back?" Mrs. Jones never replied. That brought about the sarcastic remark, "Perhaps you would rather not reply?"

As for Hannah Riley Mr. Bosanquet said, "Would it not have been kindness for you to have kept the baby?" Hannah abruptly replied, "She never asked me to take it." Mr. Bosanquet retorted, "Was your one object to get the baby out of the way so your husband would not know?" to which Hannah replied, "I did not think anything like that." In reply to further questions Hannah denied saying, "You ought to be made to get your living with the child on your back."

All the evidence concluded Mr. Bosanquet addressed the jury stating that the Prosecution had tried to make a case for deliberate murder, but he contested that his client was "so numbed by the shock of what had happened to her that she was incapable of willing anything"; she was "driven to a state bordering on hysteria and did not realise the consequences of her act".

The jury agreed and returned a verdict of manslaughter with a strong recommendation to mercy. Mr. Bosanquet then reminded the judge that the coroner's inquest had made a similar recommendation and pleaded for a light sentence as Lucy had already spent a considerable time in prison awaiting the trial.

The judge said that the recommendations of both jury and inquest enabled him to pass a less severe sentence than he should have done and would treat the case as one in which the prisoner had no intention to kill the child. He would also take into consideration the unfortunate position of the girl, but it was impossible for him not to pass some sentence of imprisonment. Therefore he had decided to pass a sentence of eight months with hard labour.

The case leaves us with some interesting questions. Why on earth was Mr. Riley kept in the dark? If told he could have hardly acted much worse than in throwing Lucy out of his home and the workhouse would have had the child in that case and Lucy as well perhaps. Why was the actual father not informed of the child? Surely Lucy knew who he was. There was never any indication of her leading an immoral life and so not knowing exactly who he was. Surely he had some responsibility for the child's upkeep and so why did Lucy not turn to him for support. Or was there some much darker secret which Lucy had to keep even from her own mother?

CHOKED TO DEATH
WIMBLEBURY 1891

After reading all the gruesome tales in the book it perhaps somewhat of a relief to discover that not all inquests into sudden deaths found that a crime had been committed and everyone involved could rest easy - all that is save for the relatives of the possible victim who might still have harboured a feeling that justice had not been done. Was that the case after the inquest into the death of young Joseph Thomas in April 1891?

On Friday April 17th Joseph arrived at his home in Glover Street, Wimblebury around half past four in the afternoon complaining of a headache and looking quite ghastly and pale. When questioned by his mother as to why he looked so ill he said that he had been set upon at work by other lads and they had almost throttled him. Feeling too ill to eat he went to bed and his mother sent for the doctor. Despite the several appearances of doctors Joseph never recovered and by ten o'clock on the Saturday he was dead.

Because of the suddenness of the death of what was in all appearances a very healthy lad the police were called and the order for a post mortem and an inquest was set in motion. That inquest was held at the Lamb and Flag Inn on Tuesday April 21st before the Deputy Coroner, Mr. H. Jordan, with Mr. Thomas Evans from Church Hill in attendance for the Cannock and Rugeley Colliery Company. The jury, after being sworn in, were taken to see the body and then all returned to the room in the public house set aside for the hearing.

*It was quite possible that the body was in another room in the public house awaiting the inquest. For those who read my book *"A History of Hednesford and Surrounding Villages"* you will remember that the Cross Keys had a corpse of a miner in an upstairs room when a group of men, wanting to carrying on gambling, simply moved it to one side while they set up their cock fighting ring.

71. The Lamb and Flag today. Little has changed of the frontage save for the addition of a porch.

Mrs. Eliza Thomas, a widower, was first to take the stand. She said that her son was a healthy fifteen year old lad who worked at the Wimblebury Pit as a pit pony driver. (His fifteenth birthday had been on the very day that he had been taken ill.) On that day he left for work just before seven o'clock and looked "well and hearty". He returned home at around four thirty and when she noticed him, having come out of her shop at the front, he was sitting at the table with his head in his hands. All that he could say was "My head" which he kept repeating.

She noticed that his right ear looked "ghastly white" and thinking that he had a headache she mixed him some medicine. When she asked him what the matter was he said, "My head hurts and it is cold," and held it close to the fire. He then said, "They have throttled me till I could not see." He then went on to say that a chap called "Mackrell" had throttled him then had shaken him and finally had thrown him against the pit

126

side. He could not tell her why it had happened because he had not sworn at him or given him any other cause to do what he did. She then asked him when it had happened and he said about quarter past three, but he had continued to work until the shift was over. As to how he managed to get home he said that it was difficult as he could hardly see where he was going.

When she questioned him further her son told her that Ingram (Mackrell's actual surname) took his knife off him, swore at him, got hold of his whip and would not let him get on with his work. At that point, having put her son by the fire, she went to see Mr. Atkins, the underground manager, to ask him to come and look at her son. He said he would if it was "necessary" and would look into the matter the next day as he did not "allow such doings".

Having returned home she put her son to bed, asked the neighbour, Mrs. Lathan, to sit with him and then went for the doctor, Mr. Holton. Finding him not at his surgery she went for Dr. Phillips at Hednesford and he gave her some medicine. However, when she got back home Joseph was in great pain and so she sent for Dr. Holton who came and examined him. During that night her son was "very thirsty and wandering". Dr. Holton was called once more and said that "he would soon be all right with a little care". About three hours later he was so ill that she sent for the doctor again. He died at about ten o'clock that night.

When questioned by the jury as to the lad's health Mrs. Thomas said that he had not been under a doctor's hands and had not missed a day's work for about eighteenth months.

Eighteen year old Alfred Talbot from Green Heath said that he was "jigging" at Wimblebury Pit and he was working at the top of the jig at half past three on the Friday. Ingram, who was nicknamed Mackrell, was on one side of him and Joseph Thomas on the other. Ingram put his hands over the witness's shoulder and laid hold of Thomas's whip. Thomas then picked something up and hit Ingram who then grabbed hold of him. However, he could not say exactly how Ingram grabbed hold of the deceased as it happened behind him. Neither could he testify as to whether Ingram struck Thomas, but the deceased did cry out.

★Young Ingram's probable first name was John, a sixteen year old lad who worked as a horse driver at the pit. However, it is just possible that it could have been his younger brother, James, who was fourteen. Both were horse drivers and lived in Wimblebury Road.

Continuing, Alfred said that Thomas then picked up a piece of rock and threatened to hit Ingram again. That stopped the quarrel. He saw the deceased about three quarters of an hour later and he did not complain of being hurt. The deceased left the pit soon after, but the witness stayed on doing some overtime.

Questioned by the jury Alfred was sure that he

72. Wimblebury Road c.1910.

saw no actual blows being struck. He had not seen them quarrel before, but had witnessed them gaming about. When asked how long they were "together" or holding each other Alfred said, "Not above a crack; not longer than you could count five." Also when questioned about the fooling about by Mr. Evans, a juryman, Alfred said, "They often had games. They came together (wrestled) whilst they were standing. It was the same everywhere he worked with young lads." Finally when asked if the deceased complained Alfred was sure that Joseph had said nothing to him.

Seventeen year old George Wright from Church Hill said that he was a driver at the pit and he was on the "fly out" near all three at the time in question. He did not see the deceased strike Ingram, but did see Ingram grab hold of the deceased "towards the neck he thought, though he could not be sure". However, he did not see Ingram shake the deceased or knock him against the side. Joseph was bending down and when Ingram let go Joseph cried out. He did not hear Joseph threaten Ingram afterwards.

Thomas went down the level after that and the witness saw him again about a quarter of an hour later "ungearing" his horse. He also remembered seeing young Joseph in the morning about 8.30 and he had then complained of having a bad throat. He also overheard Joseph telling Ingram about his throat.

When asked if Ingram had tightened the whip around the deceased's throat George said that he did not see that. At that point a juryman said, "Did anyone tell you what to say at this inquest? You seem to know very little and yet you were so close." The coroner then took up the same questioning, but all that George would say was that there was "no ill temper" though Thomas was "rather savage" as Ingram had got hold of him.

The jury were still not convinced that George was telling all that he saw and so one of them asked again, "You had got proper lamps and yet could not see what was going on. It seems very strange. Did he take the whip off him?" George finally said that he knew Ingram was pulling it, but Thomas had hold of one end of the whip.

Still not convinced the coroner recalled Alfred Talbot and asked again about the whip. Alfred simply restated that Ingram lent over his shoulder and took hold of the whip, but Thomas still held the other end. Another juryman then asked, "What brought the boy to be bending down?" Alfred then gave the rather infuriating answer "Neither were on the floor as far as he could see. Thomas did bend down to pick something up and threaten Ingram with it." The question had been neatly avoided it seemed and so the coroner dismissed Alfred.

Strangely Ingram did not appear to give evidence. He was waiting outside the courtroom, but Constable Jeffreys told the

73. Wimblebury Colliery during the 1926 Miner's Strike.

hearing that he had interviewed the lad who had made a statement to the effect that he had just caught hold of Thomas's whip to tease him. (The coroner and jury were probably satisfied that even if Ingram was forced to attend it would make little difference to anyone's version of events.)

What was to sway the jury was the evidence of Dr. Holton. (In Victorian times a doctor's evidence was considered unquestionable – strange really as medical science was nowhere near as advanced as it is today and yet we question it freely.)

Dr. Holton told the hearing that he first saw the deceased at one o'clock on the Saturday. The friends of the deceased told of the alleged incident at the pit and so he carefully examined the lad's throat, head and body and could detect no marks of violence. He knew that the lad was very ill, the cause of which he was unable to diagnose, but prescribed a simple remedy. At five o'clock he received a message to see the lad again and found him dying. A policeman who had been called to the house asked him to look for signs of injury, but again he found none save for a small one which was about four or five days old. He then left, but was again called, arriving at 9.30 p.m. to find that the boy had just died.

On Monday afternoon he carried out the post mortem which revealed minor external marks. There was a small bruise on the back of the head about the size of a two shilling piece and an old bruise with a scab on the right side. Also there was a bright bruise on the right buttock. There were no other external marks of violence.

Internally he found all the organs to be healthy except for the lungs which were in an advanced state of congestion, the right one being the worst. In his estimation it was the condition of the lungs which had caused death as they were in an advanced state of inflammation. He was surprised that the deceased could "keep on with his work in that state and his friends know nothing about it".

Questioned by the jury as to the bruising and whether it could have been a cause of the death Dr. Holton said that it "might have vaguely accelerated it". However, it was the state of the lungs which was the major cause. That had brought on a very high temperature. At five o'clock when he visited it had been 105 degrees and by seven it had reached 107 degrees. Unfortunately neither he nor Dr. Phillips had diagnosed the real problem at the time. "The last thing he thought of looking for was inflammation of the lungs."

When asked if the pains in the head which the lad had complained of would be caused by the state of his lungs the doctor said that it might be possible as "one frequent symptom of inflammation was intense headache".

All the evidence heard the coroner summed up the case. He said that "the boys had not given very satisfactory evidence" as to the scuffle which took place at the pit, but he "supposed such rough horse play was of so common an occurrence that they did not think much of it. They had no doubt consulted one another and they had stuck to their tale remarkably well." However, he thought that death was due to inflammation of the lungs. The jury agreed and a verdict of "Death according to Medical Evidence" was given.

The coroner had not finished. He thought it his duty to ask Mr. Williamson (the Company Mining Engineer) to censure the lads concerned as to their future conduct. Ingram was then ushered before the court and "severely censured" by the coroner personally.

Those lads may have been brought to their senses, but how do you stop young lads mucking about? Remember those concerned were only teenagers, most of whom would be still at school today.

Footnote:- 1. Whether Mrs. Thomas was satisfied with the verdict of the inquest was not recorded, but like many working class people in those days she would have found it far too expensive to take the case any further. Legal Aid is a very modern idea.

2. Green Heath and Church Hill were recent developments in the newly grown Hednesford and few streets had adopted names. Alfred Talbot probably lived in today's Florence Street or Ebenezer Street while George Wright probably lived in the houses at the back of St. Peter's School.

SOURCE MATERIAL

Newspapers:-

1 *Birmingham Aris Gazette*
2 *Birmingham Sunday Mercury*
3 *Cannock Advertiser*
4 *Express & Star*
5 *Staffordshire Advertiser*
6 *The Cannock Courier*
7 *Walsall Observer*
8 *Wolverhampton Chronicle*

Maps:-

1 Burntwood Tithe Map of 1845
2 Ordnance Survey Maps for 1884/5, 1902 and 1918 for the Cannock area

Parish Registers:-

1 Christ Church Parish Registers for Burntwood – Burials from 1820 – 1890
                                                   Marriages from 1845 – 1890
2 St. Luke's Parish Registers for the Cannock area – Births, Deaths and Marriages up to 1920

Census Returns:-

1 Cannock area 1871 – 1901
2 Cheslyn Hay 1861 – 1891
3 Essington 1861 – 1881
4 Heath Hayes 1871 – 1891
5 Hednesford, including Green Heath 1871 – 1901
6 Wimblebury 1871 – 1891

PREVIOUS PUBLICATIONS

ACCIDENT, MANSLAUGHTER OR MURDER?

Just who killed Thomas Hollier in a deserted lane near Burton-upon-Trent - only his faithful horse knew the answer. Was it black magic which forced the gentle John Higginson to murder his only friend? And just who was it who put the marble into the supposedly empty pistol on 5th November 1878 which killed an innocent bystander in Lichfield?

With the help of Victorian newspapers of the day, which gave vivid transcriptions of the trials, these and many other gruesome stories are retold in this, the first, of my books on murder cases in Staffordshire.

MURDERS UNSOLVED

Was it poachers who murdered young police constable Brown and dumped his body into the canal near Pendeford Bridge at Codsall? Why was 78 year old spinster, Martha Sillitoe, of Hanford so brutally bludgeoned to death in her own home? And just who was it who shot Australian Kent Reeks and left his corpse close to the bleak and disused pit mounds of the Black Country near Ettingshall?

Despite their lack of forensic science like fingerprinting or DNA the Victorian Police Force still managed to solve around 95% of all murder cases thanks mainly to the many witnesses who came forward. This book, however, delves into those few cases in Staffordshire which eluded even the most conscientious of officers and proved impossible to solve.

MURDER IN MIND

A family feud which led to death by the Llangollen Branch of the Shropshire Union Canal; a greedy son who could not wait for his father to die to get his inheritance; mistaken identity in a Ludlow hotel which almost led to the death of the wrong man; and a poisoned pie at Whixall.

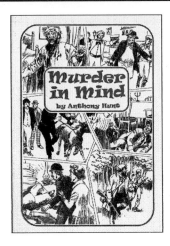

Just some of the unusual murder cases in 19th century Shropshire taken from the pages of the Shropshire Chronicle and retold in all their gory detail.

All of these books by Anthony Hunt can be bought at local shops or purchased directly from J. Roberts, The Garden House, 67 Cliffe Way, Warwick CV34 5JG or online at www.quercus.co.uk price £8.45.